westermann

CAMDEN MARKET

JUNIOR

4

W0339578

CAMDEN MARKET
JUNIOR 4

Autoren: Hannelore Debus (Mörfelden), Katrin Harder (Berlin), Amy Frances Koerner (Portsmouth), Katrin Schneider (Berlin), Elke Neudeck (Luckenwalde) sowie Phil Mothershaw-Rogalla (Prestatyn)
Unter Mitwirkung von: Daniel Harnett und Demet Kömür
Fachliche Beratung: Katrin Harder (Berlin), Mirja Anne Hommel (Frankfurt am Main), Ute Leusch (Glienicke), Katrin Schneider (Berlin)

Zusatzmaterialien zu Camden Market Junior 4

Für Lehrkräfte
- Materialien für Lehrkräfte 4 (ISBN 978-3-14-149082-4)
- Ordner für Lehrermaterialien (ISBN 978-3-14-149064-0)
- Differenzierende Kopiervorlagen 4 (ISBN 978-3-14-149083-1)
- Wort-Bildkarten 4 (ISBN 978-3-14-149084-8)
- Video-DVD 3/4 (ISBN 978-3-14-149072-5)
- Handpuppe Papagei Ruby (ISBN 978-3-425-74800-9)

Für Schülerinnen und Schüler
- Workbook 4 mit Audio-CD (ISBN 978-3-14-149078-7)
- Förderheft 4 mit Audio-CD (ISBN 978-3-14-149079-4)

Das digitale Schulbuch und digitale Unterrichtsmaterialien für Schülerinnen und Schüler und für Lehrkräfte finden Sie in der BiBox – dem digitalen Unterrichtssystem passend zum Lehrwerk. Mehr Informationen über aktuelle Lizenzen finden Sie auf www.bibox.schule.

www.westermann.de/camden-market

Druck A[4] / Jahr 2024
Alle Drucke der Serie A sind im Unterricht parallel verwendbar.

Redaktion: Daniel Harnett und Demet Kömür
Vokabelanhang: Lisa Hambrecht, Köln
Illustrationen: Ulf Marckwort, Kassel
Umschlaggestaltung: LIO Design GmbH, Braunschweig
Layout: JANSSEN KAHLERT Design & Kommunikation GmbH, Hannover
Druck und Bindung: Westermann Druck GmbH, Georg-Westermann-Allee 66, 38104 Braunschweig

ISBN 978-3-14-**149077**-0

Inhalt

Symbole

1.13	CD
3	DVD
	Partnerarbeit
	Gruppenarbeit
	Rollenspiel
	Spiel (game)
	Basteln

Kompetenz-Symbole

1.13	Hörübung (listen)
3	Hörsehübung (watch)
	Sprechübung (talk)
	Schreibübung (write)
	Leseübung (read)

	Kennzeichnung schwierigerer Aufgaben
WB 5 p.8	Übungsangebot im Workbook
WB 5 p.8	Differenzierungsangebot im Workbook
portfolio	Dokumentation gelungener Arbeiten
wordbank p.88	Bildwörterbuch

Diese Kästchen geben gute Tipps:

Viele englische Wörter sind ganz ähnlich wie im Deutschen, z. B. poster ➡ Poster
Diese kannst du dir besonders gut merken.

Ruby's tip

Tipps von Ruby

Audios und Videos: Alle Audios und Videos zum Textbook und Workbook können nach Eingabe des Webcodes **WES-149078-001** auf www.westermann.de/webcode online abgerufen werden.

Medienbildung ist an verschiedenen Stellen im Buch angelegt. In den Materialien für Lehrkräfte finden sich hierzu konkrete Vorschläge. Diese sind mit gekennzeichnet.

Back to school 1.1, 1.2

Listen and sing.

Karla

Back to school,
back to school!
Summer is ending,
back to school!

Back to the classroom,
back to my friends!
It's not so bad
when summer ends.

Back to school,
back to school!
Now it's time
to go back to school!

Rajiv

Gillian

David

Ben

1 The first day of school WB 1, 2 p.5

a) Look and listen. 1.3

Die Überschrift und die Bilder verraten dir schon viel über den Hörtext.
Schau dir beides genau an und versuche herauszufinden, worum es gehen könnte.

b) Why is Mr Cook late? Look at the pictures. Which picture do you think it is?

I think it's picture …

1

2

3

c) Listen. Which picture is correct? 1.4

2 Ruby, you're late!

a) Listen. 1.5, 1.6

b) Listen and say.

"Ruby, you're late! It's time to go!"
"Don't worry, Rajiv! I can fly, you know!"

"Ruby, you're late! Hurry up, one – two – three!"
"Don't worry, Rajiv! I can fly, you see!"

"Ruby, you're late! And I'm late, too!"
"Don't worry, Rajiv! I can fly, and you?"

c) Say it together.

3 Ruby's clocks WB 3, 4, 5 p.6, 7

a) Look and listen. 1.7

b) Listen and point.

c) Listen and say.

It's **ten** o'clock.

4 Tick tock

a) Look and listen. 1.8

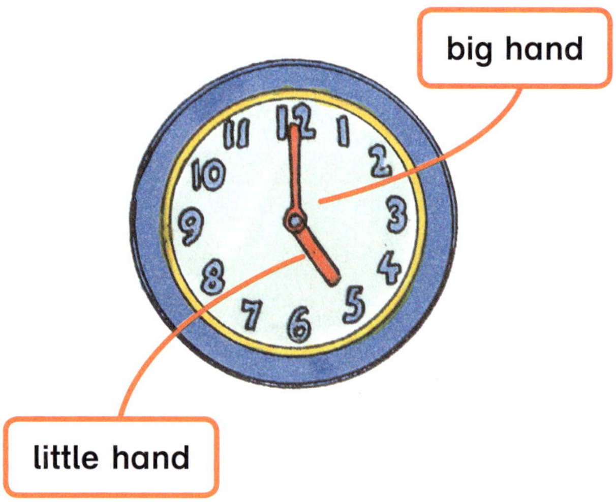

b) Listen and sing. 1.8, 1.9

c) Make YOUR song.

Tick-tock, tick-tock,
it's **one** o'clock.
The little hand's on the **one**.
The big hand's on the twelve.
Tick-tock, tick-tock,
it's **one** o'clock.

Tick-tock, tick-tock,
it's **two** o'clock.
The little hand's on the **two**.
The big hand's on the twelve.
Tick-tock, tick-tock,
it's **two** o'clock.

Tick-tock, tick-tock,
it's **three** o'clock.
The little hand's on the **three**.
The big hand's on the twelve.
Tick-tock, tick-tock,
it's **three** o'clock.

5 Clocks, clocks, clocks WB 6 p.8

a) Look and listen. 1.10 b) Listen and say.

It's four o'clock.

It's quarter past four.

It's half past four.

It's quarter to five.

Ruby's tip

It's half past four.

Es ist halb fünf.

6 Tell the time!

What time is it?
Ask your partner. Take turns.

7 What time is it?

a) Listen and read. 1.11, 1.12

b) Listen and say.

It's time to get up.
What time is it?
It's seven o'clock.
Seven o'clock?
It's seven o'clock. Hurry up!

It's time to have lunch.
What time is it?
It's half past twelve.
Half past twelve?
It's half past twelve – are you hungry?

It's time to have breakfast.
What time is it?
It's eight o'clock.
Eight o'clock?
It's eight o'clock. Hurry up!

It's time to go home.
What time is it?
It's half past three.
Half past three?
It's half past three –
come with me!

It's time to go to school.
What time is it?
It's half past eight.
Half past eight?
It's half past eight –
oh, no – we're late!

It's time to go to bed.
What time is it?
It's half past seven.
Half past seven?
It's half past seven –
off to bed!

c) Act it out.

8 What's the time Mr Wolf? 1

a) Watch. What can you see?

b) Play the game.

c) What other playground games do you play?

I play …

9 Rajiv's day WB 7, 8 p.8, 9

a) Listen and point. 1.13 b) Listen and say.

10 Issam's day

a) Read. b) Talk about YOUR day.

I get up at …

I get up at **quarter past seven**.
I have breakfast at **half past seven**.
I go to school at **half past eight**.
I have lunch at **half past twelve**.
I go home at **half past three**.
I do my homework at **four o'clock**.
I have dinner at **seven o'clock**.
I go to bed at **eight o'clock**.

c) What about YOUR Saturday or Sunday? WB 9 p.10

10: wordbank p.86

Land und Leute ▷2

Big Ben

Die berühmteste Uhr Großbritanniens ist *Big Ben*. *Big Ben* ist eigentlich der Name der größten Glocke im Uhrturm, aber viele Leute nennen auch den Turm so. Seit Juni 2012 heißt der Turm offiziell *Elizabeth Tower*, benannt nach *Queen Elizabeth II*.

Die Glocke *Big Ben* wiegt 14,5 Tonnen – mehr als zwei afrikanische Elefanten! Für die 334 Stufen hinauf zur Glocke braucht man etwa eine Stunde. Aber nur die Einwohner von London dürfen den Turm besteigen.

Wo gibt es bedeutende oder große Uhren in deiner Gegend?

Sieh dir den Clip an. Könntest du dir vorstellen, dort oben zu stehen?

11 The six-dinner cat

a) **Listen to the story.** 1.14

b) **What can you say about Sammy?**

Choose portfolio

▲ **Make a funny clock. Present it.**

● **Make time cards. Play bingo.**

■ **Find out what time it is now in Sydney, Paris and Los Angeles.**

1 What time is it?

a) Answer the questions.

b) Make YOUR quiz for a partner.

You go to school at half past eight.
Four hours later you have lunch.
What time is it?

You go home at half past four.
Four hours later you go to bed.
What time is it?

2 Ruby's day

a) Find the clocks.

b) What time is it?

In picture 1 it's …

3 The White Rabbit

a) Listen. 1.15

b) Listen and say.

The White Rabbit

I'm late, I'm late,
for a very important date.
No time to say "Hello", "Goodbye".
I'm late, I'm late, I'm late!

from *Alice in Wonderland*

4 Detective

When does Issam go to bed?

Auf den Test Yourself-Seiten im Workbook kannst du überprüfen, was du in *Theme* 1 gelernt hast.

1 ⊞

1+ Welcome to my day!

a) **Watch.** ▷ 3

I get up at quarter to seven.

At quarter past twelve I have lunch.

I go home at quarter past three.

b) **Read.**

At seven o'clock I have breakfast with my mum.

At half past eight I go to school.

At eight o'clock I go to bed.

1

2

3

4

5

6

c) **Match the sentences with the photos.**

d) **Make a video or photo story about YOUR day.**

WB 1+ p.13 portfolio

2+ Days, weeks, months, years WB 2+, 3+ p.14

a) Look and read.

b) Find the right order.

There are **sixty seconds in a minute**.

There are …

- 60 seconds
- 60 minutes
- 24 hours
- seven days
- four weeks
- twelve months

- in a week.
- in a day.
- in a month.
- in a year.
- in an hour.
- in a minute.

3+ In one minute

a) What can you do in one minute?

You need: a stop watch

How many times can you **hop on one leg**?

How many times can you **click your fingers**?

How many times can you **write your name**?

How many times can you **bend your knees**?

How many times can you … ?

b) Make a list.

How many times can you...

	... hop on one leg?	... click your fingers?	... bend your knees?	... write your name?
Leni	100	115	64	25
Abdel	108	104	65	23
Milo	72	106	78	20
Erik	103	119	160	24
Meyra	102	90	50	14

1 A school club for David

a) What are your hobbies?

b) Look and listen. 1.16

My hobby is …

I like …

c) Listen again. What does David think about football club, art club and gardening club?

Es gibt viele Wörter, die im Englischen und Deutschen ähnlich sind. So heißt z. B. das englische Wort „planet“ auf Deutsch „Planet“. Achte auf diese Wörter. Sie helfen dir, einen Text besser zu verstehen.

2 The perfect school club

a) What is the perfect school club for David? Listen again to the children. 1.16

1

science club

2

football club

3

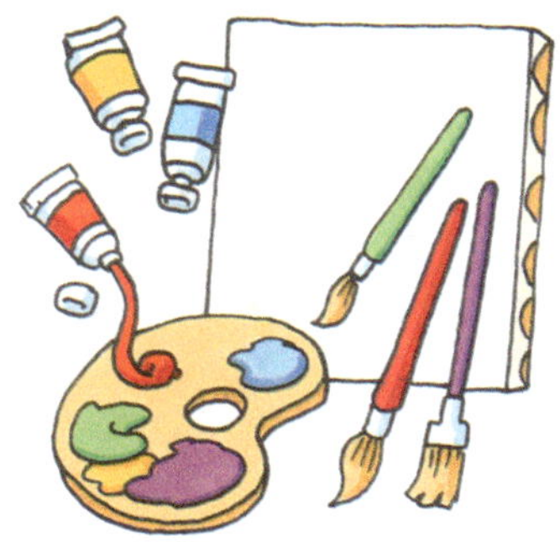

art club

b) What do YOU think? Talk to your partner.

What is the perfect school club for David?

... is the perfect school club for David.

c) Now listen to Gillian. What is her idea? 1.17

3 School clubs WB 1–5 p. 15–17

a) Look and listen. 1.18 b) Listen and say.

computer club

drama club

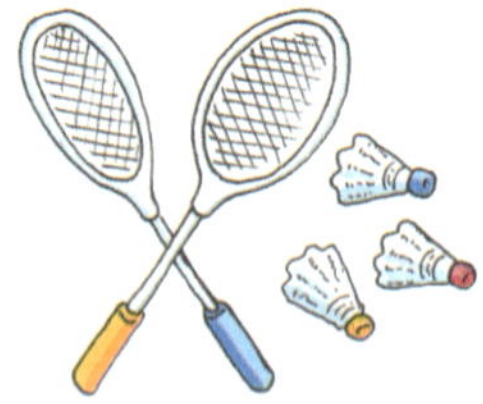

badminton club

choir

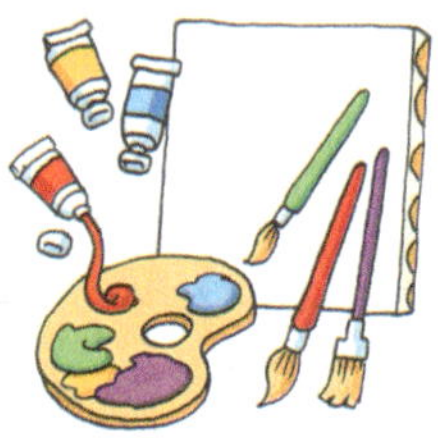

art club

music club

gardening club

dance club

c) Talk in class.

Do you go to a school club?

Yes, I go to …

No, I don't go to a school club.

d) What is the perfect school club for YOU?

… is the perfect school club for me.

3: wordbank p. 87

4 Football club WB 6 p.18

a) Listen and read the text. 1.19

Hi, my name is Leyla. I go to football club every Tuesday. Our coach is a very good football player. He shows us lots of tricks!

We work hard at football club: we run around and we dribble, head and pass the ball.

In the pictures you can see me and my friend Noyan. He's the one in the goal and he is a fantastic goalkeeper!

You can see our football kit, too – our football shirts are orange and our shorts, socks and football boots are black. Look – I'm number 5!

Football club is so much fun!

b) When is football club?

c) What are the friends wearing?

The friends are wearing …

5 Come to basketball club!

a) Watch. 4

b) Where do the children play basketball?

c) When is basketball club?

d) Make a video or poster about YOUR school club.

6 At science club WB 7 – 9 p. 18, 19

a) Listen and read. 1.20

David is at science club.
They are doing a project
about space and planets.

Mr Baxter: OK, there are eight planets. Our planet's name is …
Tim: Earth!
Mr Baxter: Very good. We live on planet earth. And you all know that the earth turns around.
Sue: Once a day!
Mr Baxter: Very good, the earth turns around once a day. So we have day and night.
David: And the earth goes around the sun.
Mr Baxter: Yes, very good, David! The earth goes around the sun once a year! And what goes around the earth?
David: The moon!
Mr Baxter: Well done, yes. So, the earth turns around and goes around the sun. And the moon goes around the earth. Let's read about the moon …

b) What planet are they talking about?

c) Read to your partner.

The  turns around.

The  goes around the  .

The  goes around the  .

d) Do you know other planets?

6: wordbank p. 88

7 The moon WB 10 p.20

a) Listen and read. 1.21

The moon goes around the earth once a month. The moon looks very small in the sky at night. It looks so small because it is so far away. The moon is very hot in the day and very cold at night.

The moon does not always look the same in the sky. As the moon goes around the earth, it looks different. Sometimes it looks like there is no moon. This is called a new moon. After that the moon gets bigger and bigger. When the moon is round and bright, it is called a full moon.

New moon means no moon.

The first man on the moon

It's July 1969.
Neil Armstrong, an astronaut from the USA, lands his space shuttle *Apollo 11* on the moon.
He is the first man to "walk" on the moon.

b) What do you find interesting?

c) Make a fact file or a poster about the moon.
Write down four interesting things. Present.

Land und Leute ⊙5

School clubs in Großbritannien

An den meisten britischen Schulen gibt es *school clubs* (Arbeitsgemeinschaften/AGs). Diese finden entweder in der Mittagspause oder nach dem Unterricht statt. Die Schüler entscheiden natürlich selbst, ob sie zu einem *school club* gehen und bei welchem sie mitmachen möchten.

Jeder kann etwas finden, das ihn interessiert: Die Kinder haben die Möglichkeit, Teamsportarten kennenzulernen und gegen andere Schulen zu spielen. Wer gerne singt oder ein Instrument spielt, kann im Chor oder Orchester üben und vielleicht sogar beim Tag der offenen Tür (*open day*) oder am Ende des Schuljahres vor Publikum auftreten.

Es gibt aber auch ungewöhnlichere *clubs*, beispielsweise den *animation club*. Dort lernen die Schüler zum Beispiel, wie man Videoclips macht.

Wie ist das an deutschen Schulen?

Sieh dir den Clip an. Worüber würdest du einen Film drehen?

8 David in space

a) Listen to the story. 1.22

b) What is David's dream about?

Choose portfolio

▲ **Find out on the Internet about school clubs at Baddow Hall Junior School.**

● **Look at page 19. Make a mini football dictionary.**

■ **Interview the alien from David's dream.**

1 Which school club?

Look. Which school club is it?

It's …

2 The earth turns around

a) Listen. 1.23, 1.24

b) Listen and sing.

The  turns around. The  turns around.

Once a day, every day, the  turns around.

The  goes around the  . The  goes around the  .

Once a month, every month, the  goes around the  .

The  goes around the . The  goes around the .

Once a year, every year, the  goes around the .

3 Ruby's tongue twisters: space

a) Listen. 1.25

b) Listen and say.

The sun and the stars look so small in the sky.

Six spaceships race to space.

Paint a pretty picture of a pink and purple planet.

4 Detective

Which planet can you see on page 16?

Auf den **Test Yourself**-Seiten im Workbook kannst du überprüfen, was du in *Theme* 2 gelernt hast.

1+ Planets WB 1+, 2+, 3+ p.23, 24

a) Read the text.

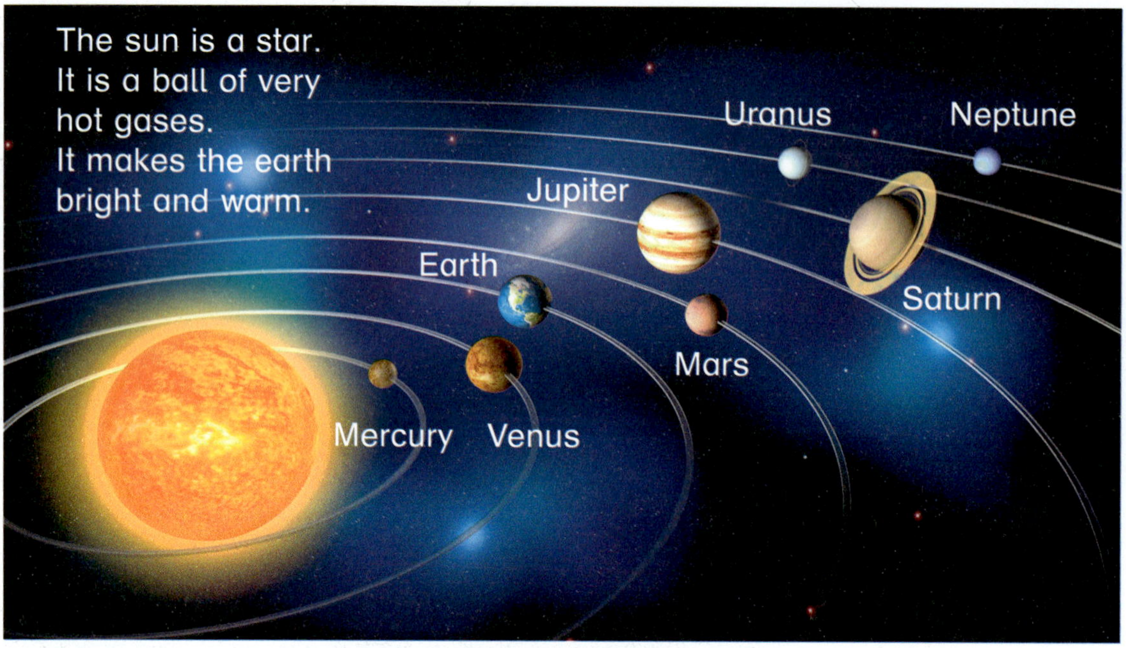

There are eight planets in our solar system:
Mercury, Venus, Earth, Mars, Jupiter, Saturn, Uranus and Neptune.
The sun is the centre of the solar system. All planets go around the sun.

Mercury and Venus are Hot planets. They are close to the sun.
The other planets are far away. They are Cold planets.

There are rocky planets and gas planets.

Mercury, Venus, Earth and Mars are rocky planets.	Jupiter, Saturn, Uranus and Neptune are gas planets. Saturn has got a ring.

b) How many gas planets are there?
How many rocky planets are there?

There are … planets.

c) Choose a planet. Present it. WB 4+ p.24

2+ Night and day

a) **Read the text.**

Day and night happens because the earth turns around. This takes one day (24 hours).

One side of the earth looks at the sun. On this side it is daytime.

The other side looks away from the sun. On this side it is dark and it is nighttime.

b) **Tell your partner what you understand.**

c) **Do the experiment.**
You need: a dark room, a torch, a sticker and a ball or globe.

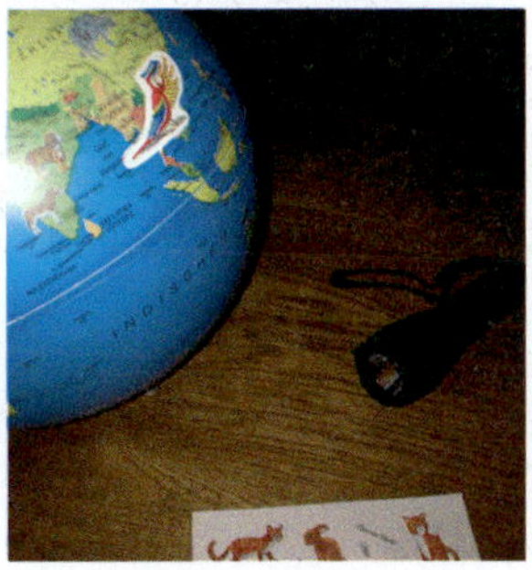

1 Karla is excited! WB 1 p.25

a) Look at the picture.

Why is Karla excited?

b) Listen. Which month is it? 1.26

c) Say the months of the year.

2 When is YOUR birthday? WB 2 p.25

Talk to your partner.

My birthday is in March. When is your birthday?

My birthday is in …

1, 2: wordbank p.89

3 Birthday ideas WB 3 p.26

a) Look. What are Karla's ideas for her birthday?

Karla would like to …

b) Listen to Karla and her mum. 1.27

c) Listen again.
What is her mum's idea?

4 Birthdays WB 4 p.26

a) Listen. 1.28

b) Listen and say.

go swimming

go to the cinema

go to a museum

go to the zoo

have a party

play party games

c) What would YOU like to do?

On my birthday
I would like to …

4: wordbank p.89

5 A birthday invitation WB 5, 6 p.27

a) Look and listen. 1.29

b) When and where is Karla's party?

Karla's party is on …

c) Listen again. What would Karla like for her birthday?

Karla would like … for her birthday.

d) What would YOU like for your birthday?

I would like … for my birthday.

6 Birthday words

a) Look and listen. 1.30

b) Listen and say.

birthday cake

balloons

birthday cards

candles

presents

c) What other birthday words do you know?

6: wordbank p.88

7 Karla's birthday party WB 7, 8 p.28, 29

a) Look at the pictures. What can you see?

b) Listen. 1.31

c) What is Sarah's present for Karla?

There is a basketball.

There are …

Ruby's tip

There is one friend.

There is one present.

There are seven friends.

There are four presents.

8 Let's talk about birthdays!

a) Watch. 6

b) What do the children like about birthdays?

c) What do YOU like about birthdays?

9 Birthday song

a) Listen and read. 1.32, 1.33 **b) Listen and sing.**

B is for birthday cake, birthday card, balloon.

I is for invitation – can you come? Tell me soon!

P is for party and presents for me.

C is for candles – blow them out: 1, 2, 3!

c) Do you know birthday songs in other languages?

Land und Leute 7 WB 9 p.29

Partyspiele in Großbritannien

Wie überall gehören auch in Großbritannien Spiele *(party games)* zum Kindergeburtstag dazu. Gerne wird *Musical chairs* gespielt, das ihr vielleicht als „Die Reise nach Jerusalem" kennt.

Ein anderes Spiel is das *Chocolate bean game*. Auf dem Tisch werden einige Schokolinsen verteilt. Jedes Kind erhält ein Trinkröhrchen und einen Becher. Mit dem Trinkröhrchen soll es die Schokolinsen ansaugen und in seinen Becher fallen lassen. Erst wenn die Linsen im Becher gelandet sind, dürfen sie mit den Händen berührt und gegessen werden.

Beliebt ist auch *Pass the parcel*. Bei diesem Spiel sitzen alle Kinder im Kreis. Im Hintergrund spielt Musik, und ein Päckchen wird herumgereicht. Das Päckchen besteht aus vielen Schichten, die jeweils eine Süßigkeit oder ein anderes kleines Geschenk enthalten. Wenn die Musik stoppt, darf das Kind, das das Päckchen gerade in der Hand hält, die äußerste Schicht auspacken und das Geschenk behalten.

Was spielt ihr auf einer Geburtstagsfeier?

Sieh dir den Clip an. Beschreibe das Spiel *Pin the tail on the donkey* in deinen eigenen Worten.

10 A very special day

a) Look at the pictures. What do you think the story is about?

b) Look and listen. 1.34

c) Listen again. Tell your partner what you understand. WB 10 p.30

Du kannst auch einzelne Wörter nennen, die du verstanden hast.

11 Liam's birthday surprise WB 11 p.30

a) Listen to the story. 1.35

b) What is the problem?

c) What can Liam and his guests do?

Du kannst dir Wörter besser merken, wenn du viele Wörter und Ausdrücke zu einem Thema sammelst und sortierst. Das kannst du zum Beispiel mit einem *word web* machen.

Choose portfolio

▲ Make a birthday party word web.

● Find out more party games in Great Britain and tell the class.

■ Make a collage of your dream birthday. Present it to the class.

Choose: wordbank p. 88, 89

1 A birthday chant

a) **Listen and read.** 1.36, 1.37

b) **Read it together.**

c) **Make YOUR chant.**

It's my birthday!
It's my birthday!
What would you like?
What would you like?
I'd like a party.
I'd like a party,
a party with lots of friends!

2 Ruby's birthday

a) **What birthday things are there in the picture?**

There is …

There are …

b) **What other things can you see?**

3 Ruby's tongue twisters: dinosaurs

a) **Listen and read.** 1.38

b) **Listen and say.**

Dan, the Diplodocus, dances every day in December.

There's tea for T-Rex and tomatoes for Triceratops.

4 Detective

How old is Karla now?

Auf den Test Yourself-Seiten im Workbook kannst du überprüfen, was du in *Theme* 3 gelernt hast.

1+ Meet the dinosaurs

a) **Listen.** 1.39

b) **Read.**

Tyrannosaurus Rex

Hello! I'm Tyrannosaurus Rex
but you can call me T-Rex.

I'm big. I'm 15 metres long and
I weigh six tons.
I've got a long, strong tail, two long legs
with strong claws and two short arms.

I walk on two legs.
I've got 58 sharp teeth and I eat meat!
I'm the king of the dinosaurs!

c) **Listen.** 1.40 d) **Read.**

Triceratops

Hello! I'm Triceratops.
I'm nine metres long from head to tail.
I'm strong. I can fight the T-Rex with
my long, sharp horns!

I've got three horns and flat teeth.
I've got a big head, a short tail and
short legs.

I walk on four legs. I eat plants.
I lay big eggs.

e) **Make a fact file for the T-Rex or the Triceratops.** WB 1+ p.33

2+ A day at the museum WB 2+ p.34

a) **Look at the pictures of Thomas and Catherine's day at the museum.**

b) **Listen and read.** 1.41, 1.42

Catherine: There are some really interesting things at Dinosaurland. My favourite thing is a model of a baby Triceratops. It's so cute! There is also some dinosaur poo. The poo weighs 73 kilos and is about 160 million years old. That's really old poo! There are dinosaur eggs, too.

Thomas: Dinosaurland is great! There are lots of dinosaurs to see at the museum – dinosaurs that fly, dinosaurs that swim and dinosaurs that live on land, like the Megalosaurus. What a good name! There is a museum shop, too. – I like the toy dinosaurs!

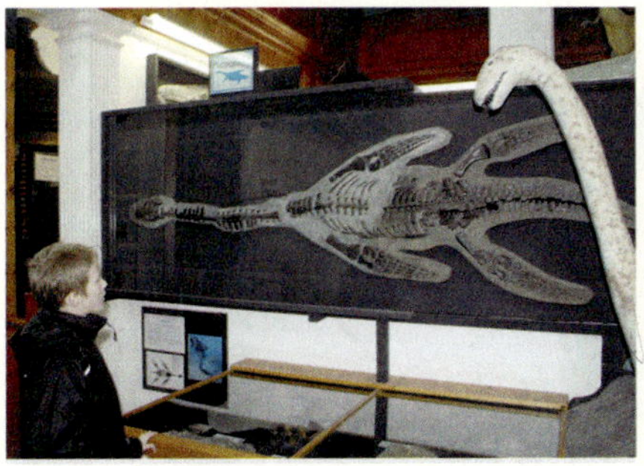

c) **What do YOU find interesting?**

1 At the supermarket

a) Look at the pictures for one minute.
Close your book. Which food words can you remember?

b) Look and listen. 1.43

c) **Listen again. What is in the trolley in the end?**

d) **Act out the dialogue.**

2 Trolley chant WB 1 p.35

a) **Listen to Karla's mum.** 1.44, 1.45

b) **Listen and say.**

What's in the trolley,
what do you see?
Orange juice and carrots
for you and me.

What's in the trolley,
what do you see?
Broccoli and fish
for you and me.

c) **Make Karla's trolley chant.**

What's in the trolley,
what do you see?
...

2: wordbank p.90

3 What we eat and drink WB 2, 3 p.35, 36

a) Look and listen. 1.46

b) Listen and say.

muesli

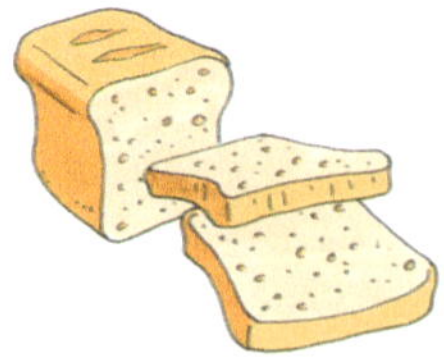
bread

yoghurt

lemonade

carrots

ice cream

nuts

broccoli

water

crisps

sweets

milk

c) What do we eat? What do we drink?
Make a list.

d) Find more words in a dictionary. WB 4 p.36

Ruby's tip

	chips	Pommes frites
	crisps	Chips

3: wordbank p.90

4 Often, sometimes, never WB 5 p.37

a) Watch. 8

b) What do the children often eat?
What do the children sometimes eat?
What do they never eat?

c) Talk to your partner.
What do YOU eat?

4: wordbank p.90

5 Let's go shopping! WB 6 p.38

a) Watch. 9

b) What is on the shopping list?

c) What else do Rhys and his mum buy?

6 Numbers WB 7, 8 p.38, 39

a) Look and listen. 1.47

11	eleven
12	twelve
13	thir**teen**
14	four**teen**
15	fif**teen**
16	six**teen**
17	seven**teen**
18	eigh**teen**
19	nine**teen**

20	twenty
30	thirty
40	forty
50	fifty
60	sixty
70	seventy
80	eighty
90	ninety

21	twenty	-one
22		-two
23		-three
24		-four
25		-five
26		-six
27		-seven
28		-eight
29		-nine

b) Listen and say. 1.48

20	11	72
64	43	50

Nenne erst die Zehner-Zahl, dann die Einer.
23 heißt twenty-three.

Ruby's tip

British money

In Großbritannien bezahlt man mit *pounds* (£) und *pence* (p).

50p = 50 pence
£1 = one pound
£5 = five pounds
£1.50 = one pound fifty

6: wordbank p.91

7 At the farmer's market

a) Look and listen. 1.49

b) What does Ben's grandma buy?

8 Shopping dialogue

a) Read the shopping dialogue with a partner.

Hello.

Hello.

Can I help you?

Yes, I'd like **four apples**, please.

Anything else?

No, thank you. How much is that?

That's **one pound ninety**, please.

Here you are.

Thank you. Here you are.

Thank you. Bye.

Bye.

b) Act out the shopping dialogue.

c) Act out YOUR shopping dialogue. WB 9 p.40

Can I help you?

Yes, I'd like **five bananas**, please.

Du lernst Wörter schneller, wenn du Dialoge mit einem Partner oder in einer Gruppe nachspielst.

8: wordbank p.90

Land und Leute 10

Fish and chips

Kennst du *fish and chips*? Das ist panierter und frittierter Fisch mit dicken Pommes frites. Meist kauft man dieses typisch britische Gericht zum Mitnehmen in *fish and chip shops*.
In ganz Großbritannien gibt es etwa 8500 *fish and chip shops*, die im Jahr 300 Millionen Portionen *fish and chips* verkaufen.

Die *chips* werden mit *salt* (Salz) und *vinegar* (Malzessig) gewürzt und meistens mit den Fingern gegessen.
Manche Leute essen auch gern *mushy peas* (Erbsenmus) dazu.

Kennst du ein Gericht, das typisch für dein Herkunftsland ist?

Sieh dir den Clip an. Welches typisch britische Gericht würdest du gern probieren?

9 The giant called Ed

a) Listen to the story. 1.50

b) What happens in the story?

c) Make a comic of the story.

Choose portfolio

▲ Make a menu card for your dream lunch.

● What do you need to make breakfast for a giant? Write a shopping list.

■ Write YOUR A to Z of food.

A: apple, …
B: banana, …
C: …

Choose: wordbank p. 90

1 Ruby says …

Read and say.

2 Carrots, peas and broccoli

a) Listen. 1.51, 1.52

b) Listen and sing.

Carrots, peas and broccoli,
my dad says they're good for me.
I don't think that they're so yummy.
I like chocolate in my tummy.
But if I eat my broccoli,
then there's something sweet for me.

3 Food quiz

a) Read.

1 They can be *green*, *red* or *yellow*. You can make crumble with them.

2 It's *brown*. It's sweet. It's yummy!

3 It's *orange*. It makes a good nose for a snowman.

4 It's *white*. It comes from cows. You can eat it with your muesli.

b) Find out: what food is it?

c) Make YOUR quiz.

Number 1 is …

4 Detective

What kind of ice cream does Karla choose at the supermarket?

Auf den Test Yourself-Seiten im Workbook kannst du überprüfen, was du in *Theme* 4 gelernt hast.

1+ Making a sandwich WB 1+ p.43

a) Look at the pictures and read the recipe.

This is what you need:
- bread
- butter
- a tomato
- a cucumber
- two lettuce leaves
- ham
- cheese

Wash the tomato, cucumber and lettuce.

Cut the tomato and the cucumber.

Put two slices of bread on a plate.

Spread butter on one slice of bread.

Put ham and cheese on the slice of bread.

Put slices of tomato and cucumber and lettuce on the cheese.

Put the other slice of bread on top.

Cut the sandwich.

Eat the sandwich.

b) Make YOUR sandwich.

c) Find another sandwich recipe on the Internet.

2+ Making apple crumble with Grandma WB 2+ p.44

a) Look at the photos and read the recipe.

This is what you need:

- 300 g flour
- 150 g sugar
- a little salt
- 200 g butter
- five apples

- oven temperature 180 °C

1

Weigh the flour, butter and sugar.

2

Mix the flour, sugar, salt and butter with your hands.

3

Butter the dish.

4

Cut the apples. Put the apples in the dish.

5

Sprinkle the crumble over the apples.

6

Bake it in the oven for 40 minutes.

7

Eat it hot with vanilla ice cream!

b) Apple crumble is a pudding. Find out more about English puddings on the Internet.

1 I don't feel well! WB 1, 2 p.45

a) Look at the pictures. What do you think the story is about?

b) Listen and read. 1.53

It's **Monday** morning.
Today David's class has got a test.

David: Mum, I don't feel well.
I've got tummy ache.
I can't go to school.
Mum: Hmm. OK, let's go to the doctor's then!
David: Oh … well, it's not that bad.
Mum: Good, so you can go to school!
David: OK …

It's **Tuesday** morning.
Today David's class has got a dance lesson. David doesn't like dancing.

David: Mum, I don't feel well.
I've got a headache from the test yesterday. I can't go to school.
Mum: OK, let's go to the doctor's then!
David: Oh … well, it's not that bad.
Mum: Aha, I see … then you can go to school!
David: OK …

It's **Wednesday** morning.
Today David's class has got a music lesson. David doesn't like music lessons.

David: Mum, I don't feel well. I've got really bad backache from dancing yesterday. I can't go to school.
Mum: David, you look fine.
You are going to school!
David: Oh, Mum!

Schau dir die Überschrift und die Bilder genau an und versuche herauszufinden, worum es in der Geschichte gehen könnte.

It's **Thursday** morning.
Today David's class has got a maths test.

David: Mum, I don't feel well. I've got really bad earache. I think it's from the music lesson! I can't go to school.
Mum: Stop it, David, you are OK. You are going to school!
David: Oh, Mum!

It's **Friday** morning.
Today David has got science club.
He's excited. He wakes up and …
oh, no! He has got a wobbly tooth.

Mum: David, what's wrong?
David: I've got a wobbly tooth, Mum. But I can go to school.
Mum: No, you can't go to school.
David: I haven't got toothache, Mum. And I've got science club today.
Mum: No school or science club for you today. You have got an appointment at the dentist.
David: Oh no, not the dentist!

c) Listen and read again.
What happens in the story?

On Monday
David has got …

2 What's wrong? WB 3, 4 p.46, 47

a) Look and listen. 1.54

earache

backache

toothache

> Höre dir die Wörter von der CD an und sprich sie mehrmals nach.
> Dann kannst du dir besser merken, wie man sie ausspricht.

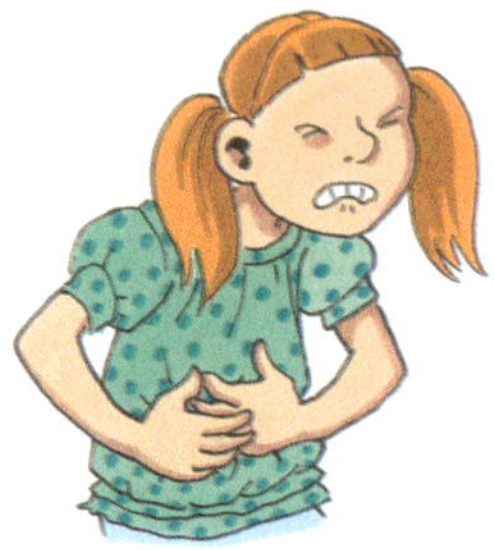

tummy ache

a headache

a cold

feel sick

b) Listen and say.

c) Talk to your partner.

What's wrong?

I can't go to school.
I've got a headache.

I can't go to school.
I feel sick.

Ruby's tip

You say **ache** like you say **make** and **cake**.

"Kate **makes** a **cake** and gets tummy **ache**."

2: wordbank p.91

3 David at the dentist WB 5, 6 p.48, 49

a) Look and listen. 1.55

b) Listen again.
What can you understand?

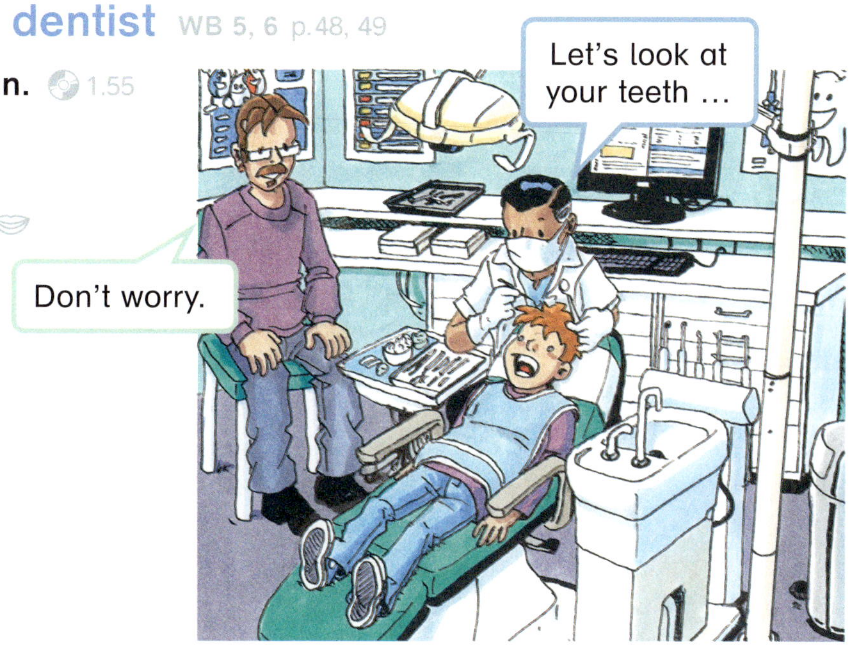

4 A brochure WB 7 p.49

a) Read.

b) What are the tips for healthy teeth? Tell your partner.

Tips for healthy teeth

Brush your teeth with toothpaste in the morning and in the evening!

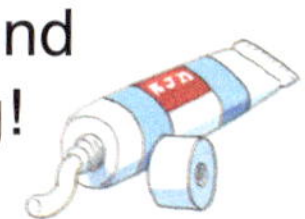

Use dental floss.

Eat fresh fruit and vegetables!
Sweets are bad for your teeth!

Drink a lot of water!
Juice or cola are bad for your teeth!

Go to the dentist every six months.

c) What is good for your teeth?
What is good for YOU? Make a poster. WB 8 p.50

Land und Leute ▷ 11

The tooth fairy

Was machen Kinder mit ihren Milchzähnen? Einige Kinder legen die Milchzähne, die ihnen ausgefallen sind, unter ihr Kopfkissen und wünschen sich etwas. Andere Kinder sammeln ihre ausgefallenen Milchzähne in einer Dose. Viele Kinder in Großbritannien schreiben einen Brief an die *tooth fairy* (Zahnfee). Für einen ausgefallenen Zahn legt die *tooth fairy* den Kindern oft ein kleines Geschenk oder Geld unter das Kopfkissen.

Was machst du mit deinen Milchzähnen?

Sieh dir den Clip an. Was machen die Kinder mit ihren Milchzähnen? Was findest du besonders interessant?

5 Captain Neverland's teeth

a) Listen to the story. 1.56

b) What are Captain Neverland's three wishes?

c) What are YOUR three wishes?

Choose portfolio

▲ **What do you like and don't you like at school? Make a list.**

I like:	I don't like:
- football club	- maths test
- music lesson	- …
- …	

● **Write a letter to the tooth fairy.**

■ **Choose a scene from "I don't feel well". Act it out.**

1 What a week!

Tell your partner. Take turns.

Gillian can't go to school on Friday.

Ben can't go to school on Thursday.

Mr Cook can't go to school on Monday.

Karla can't go to school on Wednesday.

2 Odd one out

a) What is the odd one out?

water | tummy | lemonade | cola

backache | tummy ache | sugar | earache

b) Make YOURS. portfolio

cold | dentist | teeth | toothpaste

3 Rhyming words

a) Read and say.

bread | ache | wrong | mummy | song | tummy | cake | head

b) Which words rhyme (like red – bed)?

c) Listen and check. 1.57

4 Detective

What does David's mum eat for breakfast?

Auf den **Test Yourself**-Seiten im Workbook kannst du überprüfen, was du in *Theme* 5 gelernt hast.

1+ Thomas and Catherine at the dentist WB 1+ p.53

a) Watch. 12 **b) Read.**

Dr Brookes talks to Thomas.

Thomas needs a filling.

Thomas and Catherine are at the dentist.

Dr Brookes gives the children bags with toothbrushes, toothpaste and stickers.

Now it's Catherine's turn.

The dentist calls them.

1

2

3

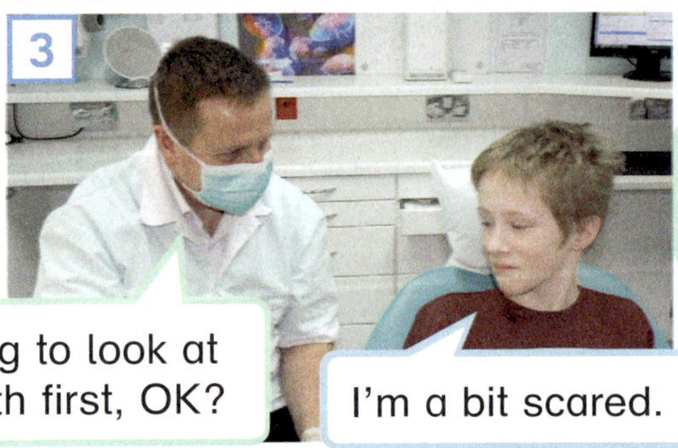

4

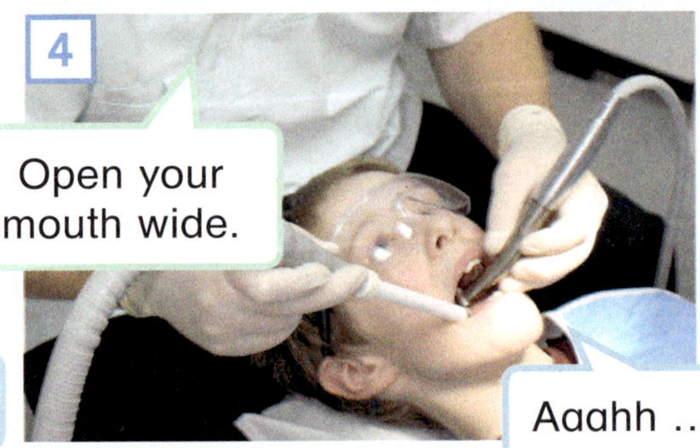

5

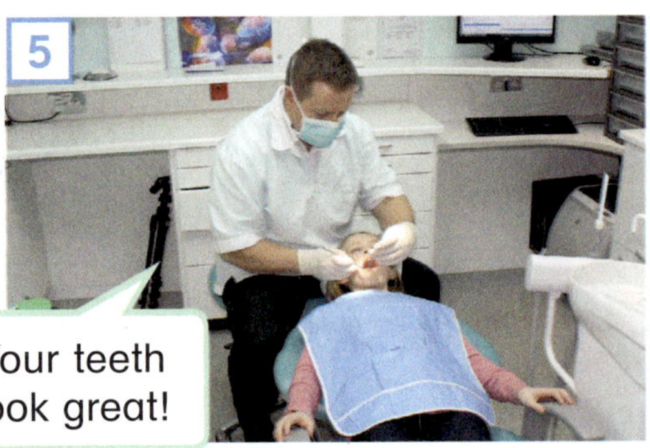

6

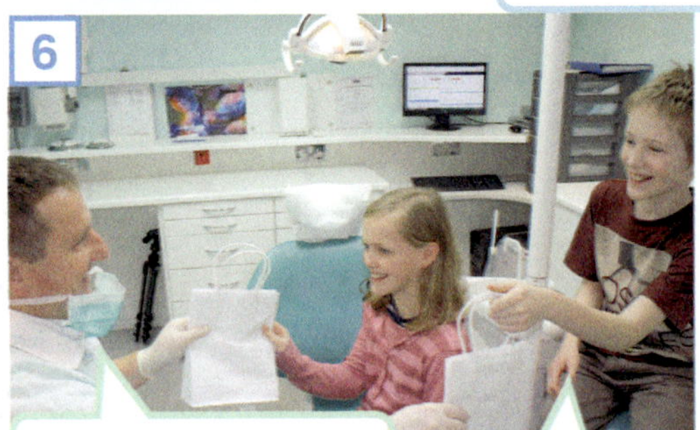

c) Match the sentences with the photos.

d) Act out the dialogue.

2+ Animal teeth WB 2+ p.54

a) Read.

Animals have got different kinds of teeth.

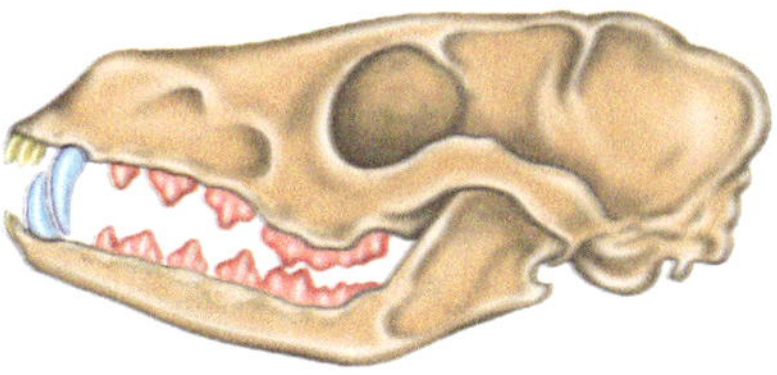

Meat-eaters have got sharp teeth.

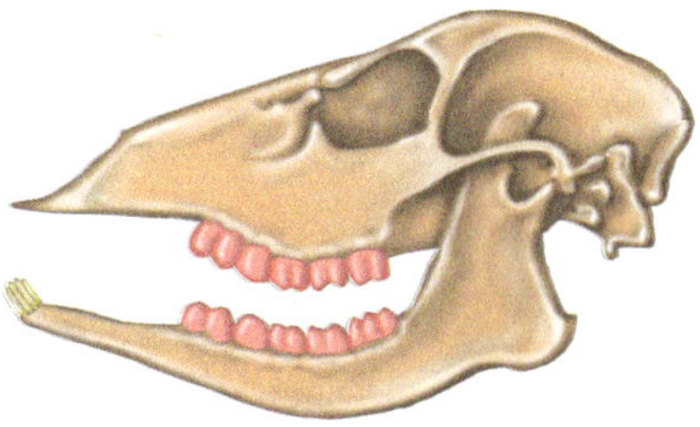

Plant-eaters have got flat teeth.

Animals that eat plants *and* meat have got sharp teeth at the front and flat teeth at the back.

Did you know that …

… dolphins have got more teeth than any other animal? Some dolphins have got more than 200 teeth. The rings on their teeth tell us how old a dolphin is.

… crocodiles have got 60 teeth in their mouths? They can grow up to 3,000 teeth in their lives.

… sharks lose teeth every week? Then they get new teeth. They can grow over 20,000 teeth in their lives.

… poisonous snakes have got hollow teeth? There is poison in the teeth!

b) Look up words you don't know. Use the word list in your book.

c) Choose an animal. Make a mini poster about animal teeth. portfolio

d) Present your poster to the class. WB 3+ p.54

1 In Ben's home WB 1 p.55

a) Look at the pictures. What do you think the story is about?

b) Listen and read. 2.1

c) Where is Ben's camera?

It's the day of Ben's class trip. He's looking for his camera in his bedroom.

Ben: Mum, where is my camera? I can't find it.
Mum: Look on your desk, Ben!
Ben: No, it's not here.
Sarah: Is it under your chair? Or under your bed?
Ben: No Sarah, it's not under my chair and not under my bed.

Now Ben is in the living room.
Ben: Mum, where is my camera?
Mum: Look on the table. Or is it on the shelf?
Ben: No, it's not here. There are only books on the shelf.

Ben is looking in the kitchen and in the bathroom. But he can't find it.

Now Ben is in the hall.
Ben: Mum, where is my camera?
Mum: Oh, Ben, look, it's here, on the chest of drawers.
Ben: Thank you, Mum!
Mum: Now hurry, you're late for the class trip.

2 In the rooms WB 2, 3 p.55, 56

a) Look and listen. 2.2

b) Listen and say.

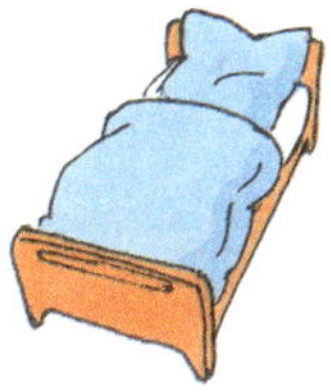

bed

chest of drawers

shelf

wardrobe

chair

desk

Schreibe die englischen Wörter für die unterschiedlichen Möbelstücke auf Klebezettel. Dann klebe den jeweils passenden Zettel, z. B. "wardrobe", an deinen Kleiderschrank. So siehst du das Wort immer, wenn du ihn öffnest, und lernst das Wort *wardrobe* praktisch nebenher.

Ruby's tip

in

on

under

3 Where is ... ?

Look at the pictures. Ask your partner.

Where is the desk?

In the bedroom.

Where are the books?

On the shelf.

2, 3: wordbank p. 92

4 At the fire station

a) Look at the pictures.
What can you see?

I can see …

There is …

There are …

b) Listen. What do you remember? 2.3

5 Fire station words WB 4 p.57

a) Look and listen. 2.4

b) Listen and say.

firefighter

fire engine

ladder

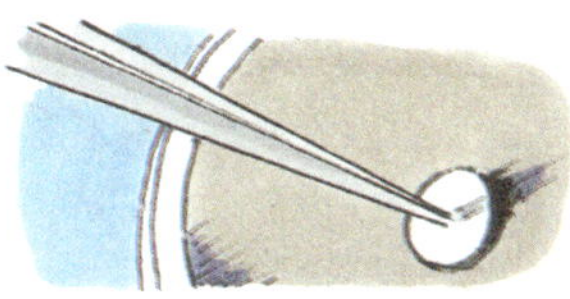
pole

garage

alarm

5: wordbank p. 93

6 What a firefighter needs WB 5, 6 p.57, 58

a) Listen and point. 2.5

b) Listen and say.

gloves

helmet

axe

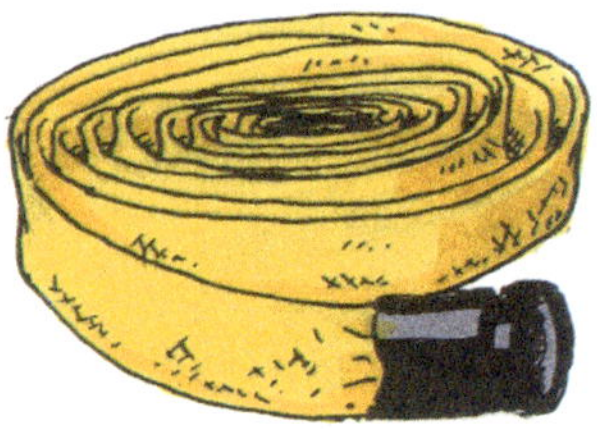

hose

torch

jacket

boots

trousers

c) Look at the firefighter. What is missing?

The firefighter has got no …

6: wordbank p.93

7 Down at the fire station WB 7 p.59

a) Listen and read. 2.6, 2.7 b) Listen and sing.

Down at the fire station, early in the morning,
you can see the firefighters **jumping out of bed**.

Down at the fire station, early in the morning,
you can see the firefighters **sliding down the pole**.

Down at the fire station, early in the morning,
you can see the firefighters **with helmets, gloves and boots**.

Down at the fire station, early in the morning,
you can see the firefighters **running to the door**.

Down at the fire station, early in the morning,
you can see the firefighters, **off to fight the fire**.

8 Inside the fire station

a) Look and listen. Follow the children through the fire station. 2.8

b) Listen again. How many firefighters work at the fire station?

c) Quiz your partner. WB 8 p.60

How many **chairs** can you see?

How many **rooms** are there?

Where is **Gillian**?

What colour are the … ?

I can see …

There is …

There are …

Gillian is in …

The … are **blue**.

8: wordbank p.92, 93

Land und Leute ⊙ 13

Notfall in Großbritannien

In einem Notfall, zum Beispiel wenn es brennt, alarmiert man die Helfer mit einem Notruf. Dazu gibt es bei uns in Deutschland die Notrufnummer 112. In Großbritannien ist die Notrufnummer die 999 oder die 112. Ein Notruf ist von jedem Telefon, auch von einem Handy, kostenlos.

Feuerwehrautos, die Polizei und auch Krankenwagen sind in Großbritannien gut zu erkennen. Oft sind die Wagen in leuchtenden Neonfarben.

Wie ist das in Deutschland? Warum werden Neonfarben benutzt?

Sieh dir den Clip an. Welche Farben haben britische Rettungswagen?

9 An experiment

a) **Look at the pictures and read.**

You need a glass, a small candle and a lighter.

Light the candle.

Put the glass over the candle and the flame.

See what happens.

b) **What happens to the flame? Find out.**

10 Freddie the firefighter

a) **Listen to the story.** 2.9

b) **Talk about Freddie's week.**

Choose portfolio

▲ **Draw a house and label the rooms.**

● **Make a fire station word web.**

■ **Make a word search about rooms and things in a room.**

K	I	T	C	H	E			
O	S	O	F	A	F	G	J	D
S	W	Z	Q	B	E	D	P	I
H	B	A	T	H	R	O	O	M
E	W	R	V	H	I	F	P	L
L	S	D	E	S	K	S	K	R
F	W	A	R	D	R	O	B	E

Choose: wordbank p. 92, 93

1 Rooms

Look. Which room is it?

Number 1 is …

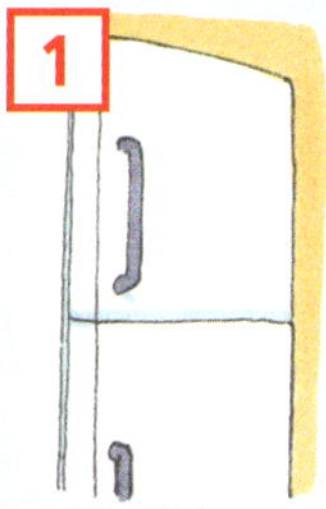

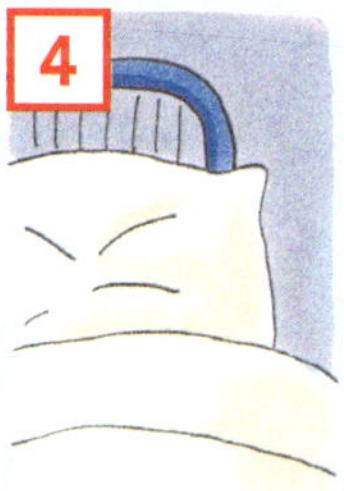

2 Things in a room

Read and find out.

1. You can sit on me. I'm a …
2. You can do your homework at me. I'm a …
3. You can sleep in me. I'm a …
4. You can put your clothes in me. I'm a …

3 Ruby's tongue twister: firefighters

a) Listen and read. 2.10

b) Listen and say.

Five fit firefighters fight five fires.

4 Firefighter words

a) Find and say the words.

b) Say all the firefighter words you know.

meehlt

otbso

tsrusroe

htocr

5 Detective

Where are Ben's coloured pencils?

Auf den **Test Yourself**-Seiten im Workbook kannst du überprüfen, was du in *Theme* 6 gelernt hast.

1+ My house

a) Watch. What rooms are there in Lauren's house? 14

b) Where is Lauren's dad? Where is Lauren's mum?

2+ My room WB 1+, 2+ p.63, 64

a) Look and listen. 2.11, 2.12

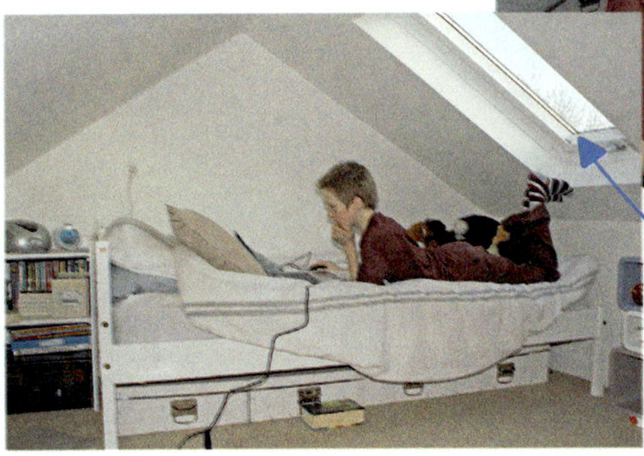

b) Choose one of the rooms. What is there in the room?

In Catherine's room there is …

c) What is there in YOUR room? Make a poster and present it. portfolio

3+ My favourite place in my room

a) Look and read.

My favourite place in my room is at my desk.
I like drawing and painting there.
I've got paper, a paintbox, pencils, pens, rulers … everything I need!

My desk is in front of a big window.
When I am at my desk
I can look out of the window and see the garden.
It's a really nice place to sit.

My favourite place in my room is on my floor.
I like sitting there and playing on my computer or with my bricks. In the photo you can see my boat and tower.

I've got lots of games in my room. Sometimes my floor is a mess. Then Mum tells me to tidy my room – I hate that!

b) What is YOUR favourite place in your room? WB 3+ p.64

1 David's street

a) Look and listen. 2.13

b) Listen again. What can you hear?

I can hear …

c) Now listen to David and his dad. Where are they going? 2.14

2 What a cool bike! WB 1 p.65

a) Look and listen. 2.15

1 brakes | 2 bell | 3 front light | 4 tyre | 5 saddle | 6 back light | 7 reflector | 8 wheel

b) Listen and say.

3 Bike chant WB 2, 3, 4 p.65, 66

a) Listen. 2.16, 2.17

b) Listen and say.

I love my bike, my B-I-K-E,
when I ride it I feel happy and free.
It's got a 
front light – back light
front reflector – back reflector
saddle and bell – saddle and bell.

It's got a
front brake – back brake 
front wheel – back wheel
it's fast as hell – it's fast as hell.
I love my bike, my B-I-K-E,
when I ride it I feel happy and free.

c) Say the chant.

4 At the bike shop WB 5 p.67

a) Look. What's wrong with David's bike?

b) Listen. Are you right? 2.18

c) Listen again. What do David and his dad buy?

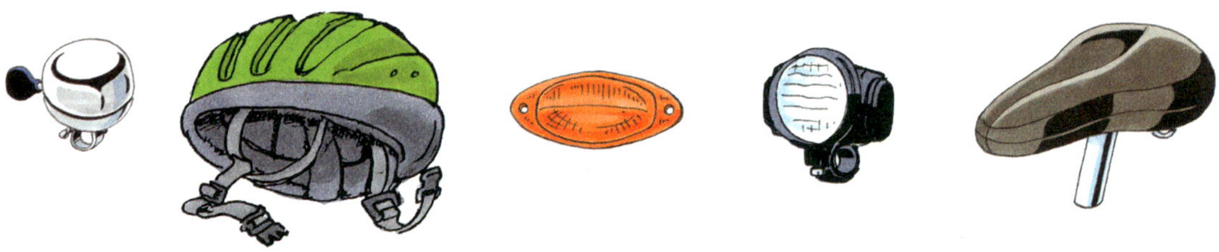

d) Present YOUR bike. Draw a picture or bring a photo. WB 6 p.68

5 A bike ride

a) Watch. 15

b) What can you understand?

c) Act out the scene.

4: Wordbank p.94

6 In the neighbourhood WB 7, 8 p.69, 70

a) Listen and read. 2.19 b) Listen and say.

swimming pool | bakery | supermarket | clothes shop | bike shop | school | park | playground | cinema | restaurant | sweet shop

c) Listen and point. Where do Rajiv, David and his dad go? 2.20

d) Listen again. When can David and his dad go swimming?

6: Wordbank p.95

Land und Leute 16

Linksverkehr in Großbritannien

In Großbritannien fahren die Fahrzeuge auf der linken Straßenseite. Das Lenkrad befindet sich bei allen Autos und Lastwagen auf der rechten Seite. Die Gangschaltung wird mit der linken Hand bedient. Natürlich sind auch Kupplungs- und Bremspedal im Fußraum auf der rechten Seite zu finden – aber in derselben Reihenfolge wie bei uns.

Wenn du in Großbritannien zu Fuß oder mit dem Fahrrad unterwegs bist, musst du also besonders gut aufpassen. Schau immer zuerst nach rechts, bevor du über die Straße gehst oder mit dem Fahrrad losfährst.

Es gibt noch mehr Länder mit Linksverkehr. Findet heraus, in welchen Ländern auch noch links gefahren wird.

Sieh dir den Clip an. Was ist in Großbritannien anders?

7 Emily's bike

a) Listen to the story. 2.21

b) Why is Emily sad?

c) Who helps Emily?

Choose portfolio

▲ **Make a mini bike dictionary.**

● **Present YOUR neighbourhood.**

■ **Make town domino cards. Play the game with a partner.**

START	You can buy sweets in the …	sweet shop	You can play in the …	playground	…

Choose: Wordbank p. 94, 95

1 What is it?

Look and say.

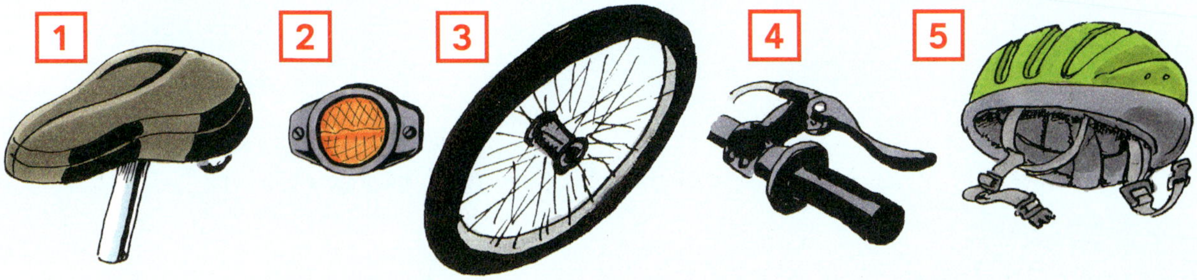

2 Eleven words

a) Read.

b) Make YOUR poem with eleven words.
Present it to your partner.
portfolio

My bike
I love it
It's fun to ride
My bike

3 Places in town

Read and answer.
Take turns.

1. Where can you **buy food**?
2. Where can you **play**?
3. Where can you **eat**?
4. Where can you **swim**?

4 Detective

Look. How many zebra crossings are there in the neighbourhood on page 69?

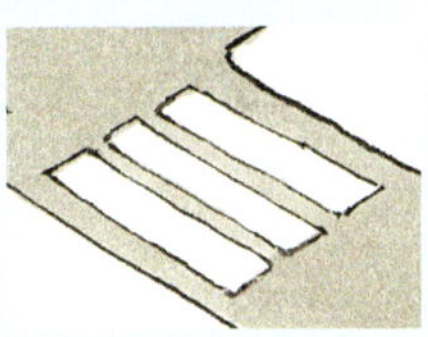

Auf den **Test Yourself**-Seiten im Workbook kannst du überprüfen, was du in *Theme* 7 gelernt hast.

1+ Places in your town WB 1+ p.73

a) What can you find in a town?
Make a word web.

b) Plan your little town.
What would you like to have in your town?

c) Choose one place.
Draw or make it.

d) Write a text about your place. portfolio

Lies den Beispieltext genau durch. Die Satzanfänge helfen dir dabei, deinen eigenen Text zu formulieren.

This is our swimming pool.
Its name is Fish Paradise.
It has got two pools and a shop.
Here you can swim.
You can buy chips.
It's open every day
from ten o'clock in the morning
until eight o'clock in the evening.

1+: Wordbank p.95

e) Present your place to the class.

f) Find a name for your town.

g) Make a flyer about your town. portfolio

Give information about:

- your town's name,
- what it looks like,
- what places there are,
- what you can do there, etc.

Draw or cut out small pictures.

h) What other things are there in your town?

bikes | cars | streets | people | traffic lights | zebra crossings | …

i) Make a poster of your town.

- Take pictures of your places.
- Stick them onto a big sheet of paper.

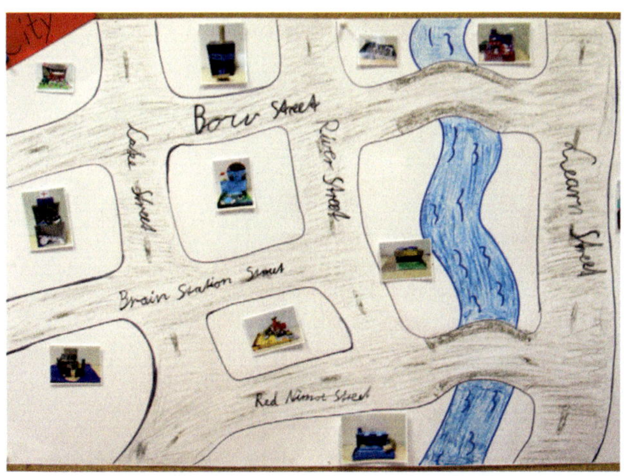

2+ People in your town WB 2+ p. 74

a) Who lives in your town? Make a character. portfolio

b) Make an information card about your character.

Name	Holly Fisher
Age I am ... years old.	I am 28 years old.
Job I am a ...	I am a chef.
Looks I have got ...	I have got brown hair. I have got brown eyes.
☺ I like ...	I like chocolate. I lke dancing.
☹ I don't like ...	I don't like shopping. I don't like cars.

c) Present your character.

Hi, my name is Holly Fisher.
I am 28 years old and
I am a chef.
I have got brown hair and brown eyes.
I like chocolate and dancing.
I don't like shopping or cars.

3+ Town festival

a) Plan a festival in your town.

Write a list for the programme.

Here are some ideas:
- a town tour
- a school open day
- games in the park
- a beach party at the swimming pool
- ...

b) How can you let people know about the festival? portfolio

Collect ideas in class. Choose:

You can make
- a poster for the festival.
- a radio jingle / advert.
- a flyer for the town tour.
- a menu for a food stall.
- ...

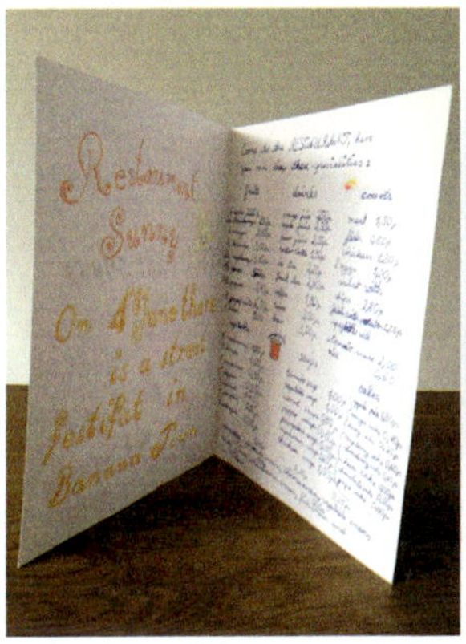

c) It is the day of the town festival. What happens?

- Some tourists come to the town festival. Plan a tour for them.
- Some people would like something to eat. Make a dialogue at a food stall.
- ...

d) Act out what happens at the festival.

1 Weather forecasts WB 1, 2 p.75

a) Look. What can you see?

b) Look and listen. 2.22–2.25

Good morning!
Here is today's weather forecast.
This morning it's going to be foggy.
This afternoon ...

autumn

foggy | windy | rainy

winter

cold | snowy | frosty

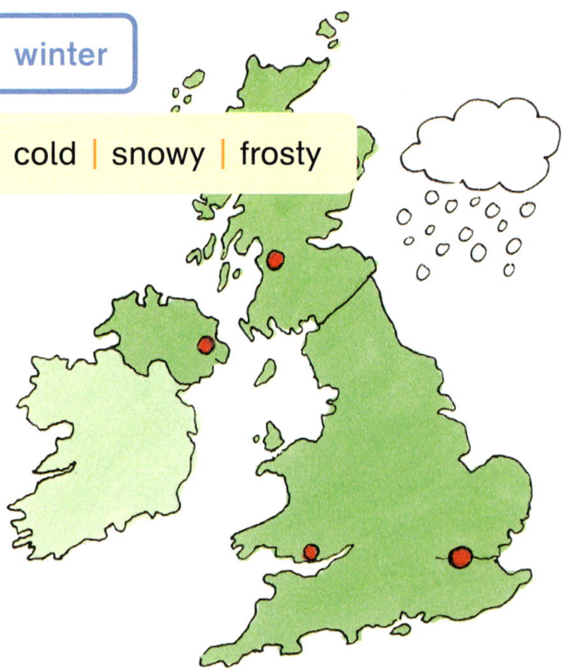

1: Wordbank p.96

c) Make YOUR weather forecast.

d) Present it.

spring

sunny | warm | rainy

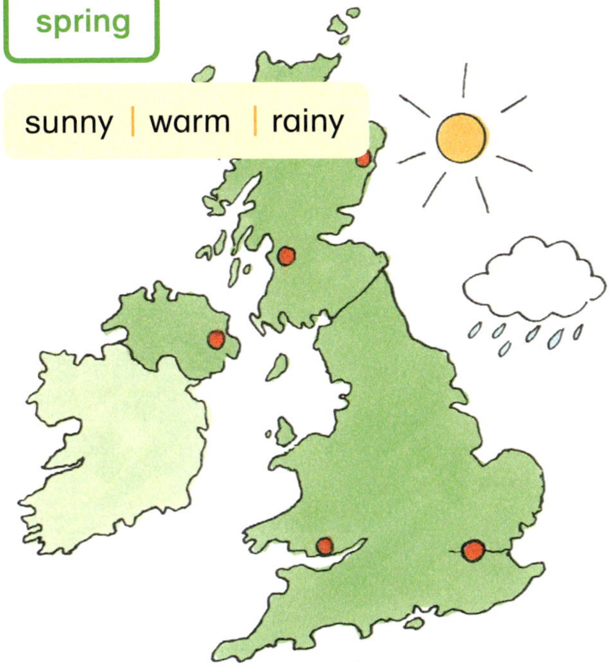

summer

sunny | dry | hot

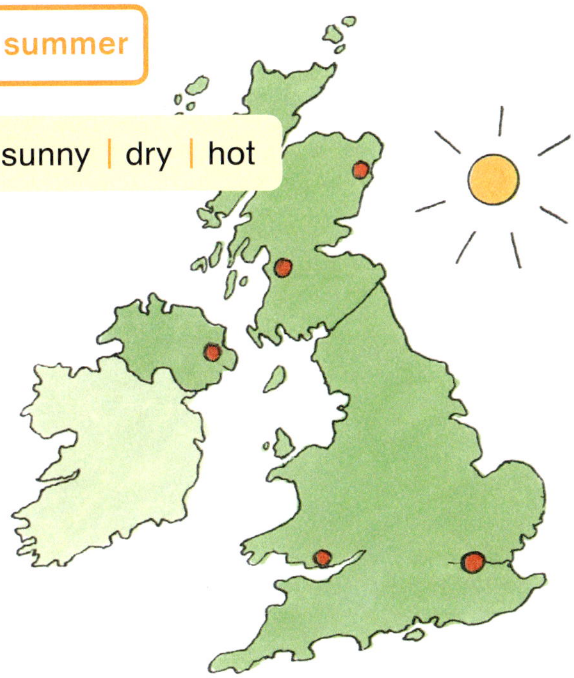

2 November

a) Listen. 2.26

b) Listen and say.

c) Present the poem.

No sunshine, lots of rain,
no warm days, snow again!
No bugs or bees,
no leaves on trees.
You must remember –
this is November!

3 We love autumn! WB 3, 4 p.76

a) Listen. What do the children like about autumn? 2.27

I love the sound of crunchy leaves.

My friends and I collect leaves and other things from trees.

I make little conker people with arms, legs and heads.

I like carving pumpkins – pumpkins with scary faces!

I wear my yellow wellies and jump in puddles.

b) Listen again and point.

c) What do YOU like about autumn?

d) Make an autumn collage.

Land und Leute 17

Bonfire Night in Großbritannien

In Großbritannien wird am 5. November *Bonfire Night* gefeiert. Dieses Fest erinnert an einen Brandanschlag auf das englische Parlament im Jahr 1605. Guy Fawkes, ein Gegner des Königs, versuchte ihn zu töten, aber der König überlebte. Um dies zu feiern, wurden in ganz England Freudenfeuer entzündet.

Bis heute wird am 5. November mit Feuerwerk *(fireworks)* und Feuer *(bonfire)* gefeiert. Auf dem *bonfire* wird eine Puppe (genannt *guy*) verbrannt, die Guy Fawkes darstellen soll. Während man das Feuerwerk anschaut, isst man oft Hot Dogs, Kartoffeln, Marshmallows und über dem Feuer geröstete Bananen.

Bei welchen Gelegenheiten wird bei uns in Deutschland ein Feuer entzündet?

Sieh dir den Clip an. Sprecht zusammen den Reim *Remember, remember.*

4 It's Bonfire Night! WB 5, 6 p.77

a) **Listen and read.** 2.28, 2.29

b) **Listen and say.**

It's Bonfire Night, what do I see?
A guy on the bonfire, looking at me!

It's Bonfire Night, what do I smell?
Hot dogs, bananas, marshmallows
as well!

It's Bonfire Night, what do I hear?
Fireworks, fireworks, loud in my ear!
Whizz. Crackle. Bang!

5 It's winter time! WB 7–9 p.78, 79

a) Listen and read. 2.30

b) Listen and say.

Class:	It's winter time!
Child:	Winter time?
Class:	Winter time!
	What do you do?
Child:	**Go ice-skating!**
	What about you?

c) What do YOU do in winter? Make YOUR chant.

go ice-skating | go skiing | play ice hockey | build a snowman | have a snowball fight | go sledging | play inside | make a snow angel | read a book | drink hot chocolate | …

6 Winter poem

a) Look and listen. 2.31

b) Listen and say.

c) Make YOURS.

Land und Leute ▶ 18

Pancake Day in Großbritannien

Pancake Day ist in Deutschland Faschingsdienstag, der letzte Tag vor Beginn der Fastenzeit. In der Fastenzeit verzichten manche Menschen ganz oder teilweise auf bestimmte Lebensmittel oder essen sogar nichts.

Früher wurden in Großbritannien an diesem Tag alle noch vorhandenen Lebensmittel aufgegessen, damit sie nicht schlecht wurden. Aus Eiern, Fett und Milch machte man Pfannkuchen *(pancakes)*. Darum heißt der Tag *Pancake Day*.

Besonders lustig ist das traditionelle Pfannkuchenrennen *(pancake race)*. Mit Pfanne und Pfannkuchen in der Hand und manchmal sogar verkleidet laufen die Teilnehmer um die Wette. Dabei muss der Pfannkuchen mehrmals gewendet werden. Das ist ein großer Spaß.

Welche lustigen Traditionen kennst du?

Sieh dir den Clip an. Esst ihr zu Hause auch manchmal Pfannkuchen?

7 A pancake party at Karla's house WB 10 p. 79

a) **Look and listen.** 2.32

b) **Listen again. How do the children like their pancakes?**

The children like their pancakes **with chocolate spread, with …**

8 Spring is here!

a) Listen. 2.33, 2.34

b) Listen and sing.

Spring is here, spring is here!
Say bye to the snow.
Spring is here, spring is here!
All the flowers grow.

Spring is here, spring is here!
Say hi to the sun.
Spring is here, spring is here!
Go outside, have some fun!

9 April fool! WB 11 p.80

a) Listen. 2.35

b) Listen and read.

Ben: Karla, today is April Fool's day.
Karla: Yes, it is. Ben, I've got an idea: let's play a trick on Mr Cook!
Ben: Great idea!

Mr Cook: Good morning, class. Please show me your homework. Yes, Ben?
Ben: Sorry Mr Cook. I haven't got my homework.
Mr Cook: Hmm. Rajiv, where is your homework?
Rajiv: Sorry Mr Cook. I haven't got my homework.
Mr Cook: Oh dear, Rajiv. Gillian?

Gillian: I'm sorry, Mr Cook, I haven't got it.
Mr Cook: Hmmm … Karla?
Karla: Sorry Mr Cook …
Mr Cook: Who is here with no homework? What? All of you? No homework? Why?
Children: April fool!
Mr Cook: Oh no …

c) Act out the story.

Land und Leute 19

Ostern in Großbritannien

In Großbritannien ist der Ostersonntag *(Easter Sunday)* der eigentliche Osterfeiertag. Neben Schokoladeneiern *(chocolate eggs)* werden auch Hefebrötchen *(hot cross buns)* gegessen. Die mit Nelken, Muskatnuss und Zimt gewürzten Brötchen sind mit einem Kreuz verziert. Das soll an die Kreuzigung von Jesus Christus erinnern. Deshalb werden die *hot cross buns* traditionell am Karfreitag *(Good Friday)* gegessen.

Ostergrüße *(Easter cards)* zu verschicken, ist auch beliebt. Ostereier suchen ist in Großbritannien nicht so stark verbreitet wie bei uns. Außerdem ist der Osterhase in Großbritannien ein Kaninchen *(the Easter bunny)*.

Wie wird Ostern in Deutschland gefeiert?

Sieh dir den Clip an. Singt zusammen das Lied *Hot cross buns*.

10 Easter at Karla's house WB 12, 13 p.81

a) Look and listen. 2.36

b) What do Karla and Grandma talk about?

11 In the summertime WB 14 p.82

a) Listen and read. 2.37

b) Listen and say.

waves

bucket

sandcastles

In the summertime,

when we've got no school,

we go to the  ,

or the 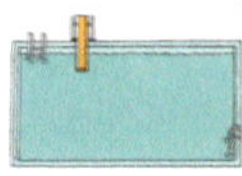 .

In the summertime,

when the weather is hot,

we wear  and 

and eat  a lot!

In the summertime,

when it's a  day,

let's play in the  ,

let's go  , we say!

In the summertime,

when it's a warm, warm day,

let's make  ,

get your  , let's play!

We love summer!

12 Plans for the summer WB 15 p.82

a) Look and listen. 2.38

b) Where is David going in the summer holidays?

c) What can you do in the summer holidays?

I can …

Land und Leute ⓟ 20

Letzter Schultag in Großbritannien

An britischen Schulen fangen die Sommerferien im Juli an und dauern etwa sechs Wochen. In der letzten Schulwoche und insbesondere am letzten Schultag sind die Kinder oft aufgeregt. Alle freuen sich auf sechs Wochen schulfrei!

An vielen Schulen werden in der letzten Woche vor den Ferien Konzerte oder Theaterstücke aufgeführt. Die Kinder spielen in den Klassen oder schauen Filme an. Am letzten Schultag gibt es manchmal sogar eine Party oder eine besondere Schülerversammlung (*assembly*) für alle. An manchen Schulen müssen die Kinder am letzten Tag auch keine Schuluniform tragen.

Was macht ihr am letzten Schultag vor den Sommerferien?

Sieh dir den Clip an. Gibt es solche Versammlungen an deiner Schule?

13 The last day of term WB 16 p.83

a) **Look and listen. What is Mr Cook's idea for the last day?** 2.39

b) **What would YOU like to do on the last day of term?**

Around the clock

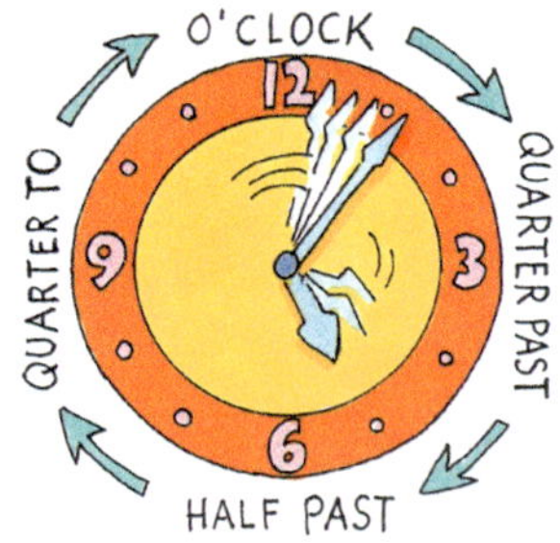

What time is it?

It's three **o'clock**.

It's **quarter past** three.

It's **half past** three.

It's **quarter to** four.

My day

I **get up** at seven o'clock.

get up

have breakfast

go to school

have lunch

go home

do homework

have dinner

go to bed

School clubs

Come to … !

gardening club

football club

computer club

badminton club

drama club

dance club

science club

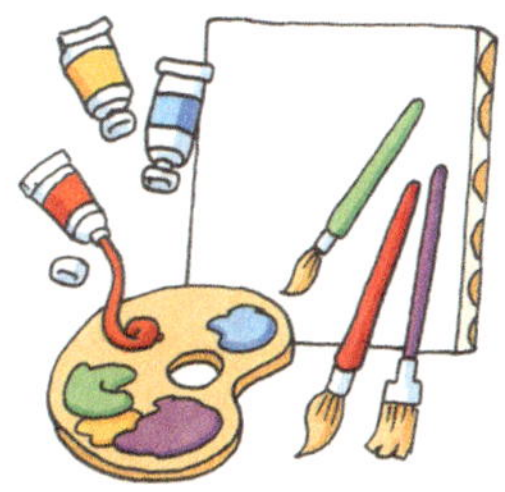

art club

book club

music club

choir

Do you go to a school club?

Yes, I go to **music club**.

No, I don't go to a school club.

Space

sun

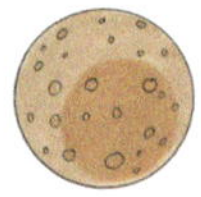

moon

earth

Earth is a planet.

The sun is a star.

The moon goes around the earth.

alien

spaceship

Birthdays

a birthday cake

an invitation

candles

birthday cards

presents

balloons

When is your birthday?

My birthday is in …

What would you like for your birthday?

For my birthday I would like **a new game**.

I would like to **eat cake**.

eat cake

HAPPY BIRTHDAY!

have a party

play party games

go swimming

go to a museum

go to the cinema

go to the zoo

Food and drink

bananas
broccoli
carrots
tomatoes

milk
water
lemonade
cola
orange juice

sweets
chocolate
ice cream
crisps
nuts

yoghurt
muesli
bread

I don't like …

Fish is good for you.

fish
chips
pizza

Shopping

1 Hello, can I help you?

2 Yes, I'd like two oranges, please.

3 Anything else?

4 No, thank you. How much is that?

5 That's one pound, please.

6 Here you are.

7 Thank you. Bye!

Numbers

11	eleven
12	twelve
13	thirteen
14	fourteen
15	fifteen
16	sixteen
17	seventeen
18	eighteen
19	nineteen

20	twenty
30	thirty
40	forty
50	fifty
60	sixty
70	seventy
80	eighty
90	ninety

21	twenty-one
22	twenty-two
23	twenty-three
24	twenty-four
25	twenty-five
26	twenty-six
27	twenty-seven
28	twenty-eight
29	twenty-nine

Ouch!

I feel sick.

feel sick

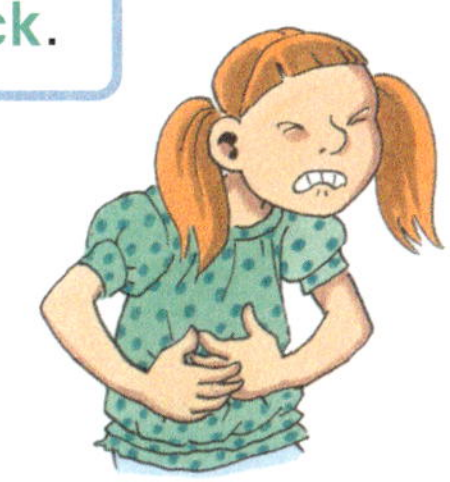

tummy ache

backache

What's wrong?

I don't feel well.
I've got a cold.

toothache

earache

a headache

a cold

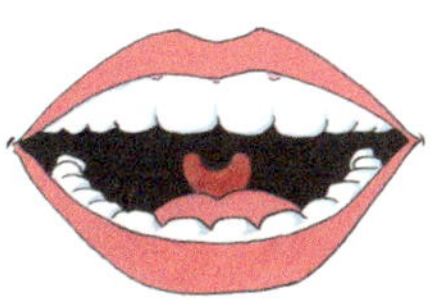

tooth / teeth

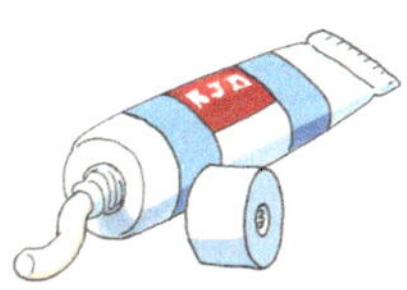

toothpaste

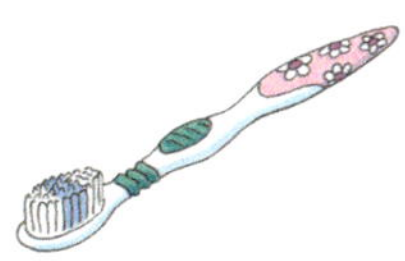

toothbrush

I brush my teeth
in the morning and
in the evening.

Rooms

living room

bedroom

kitchen

hall

bathroom

Things in a room

In my room there is a …

The books are **on** the **shelf**.

in

on

under

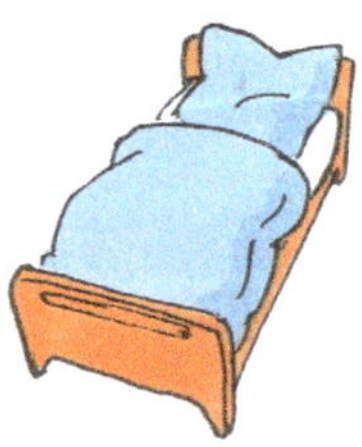

bed

shelf (shelves)

chair

desk

chest of drawers

wardrobe

At the fire station

a fire engine

a ladder

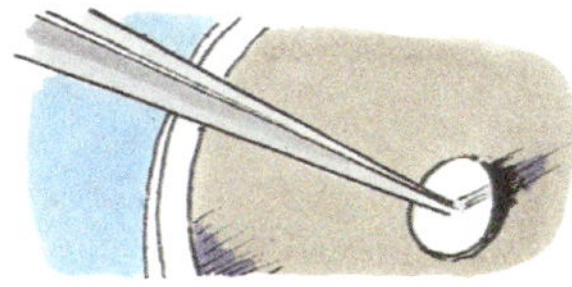

a pole

a firefighter

an alarm

a garage

What does a firefighter need?

A firefighter needs …

a torch

a helmet

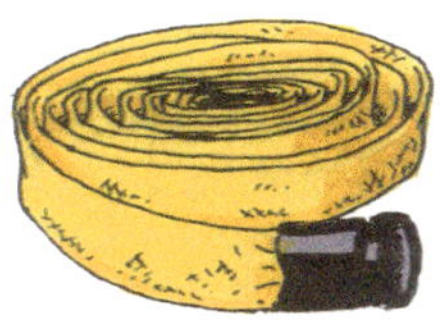

a hose

a jacket

an axe

boots

gloves

trousers

Bike

I love my bike.
saddle
back light
bell
brakes
tyre
front light
wheel
reflector

helmet
I need to repair my tyre.
I'd like to buy a new saddle.
Stop, you need your helmet!

Places

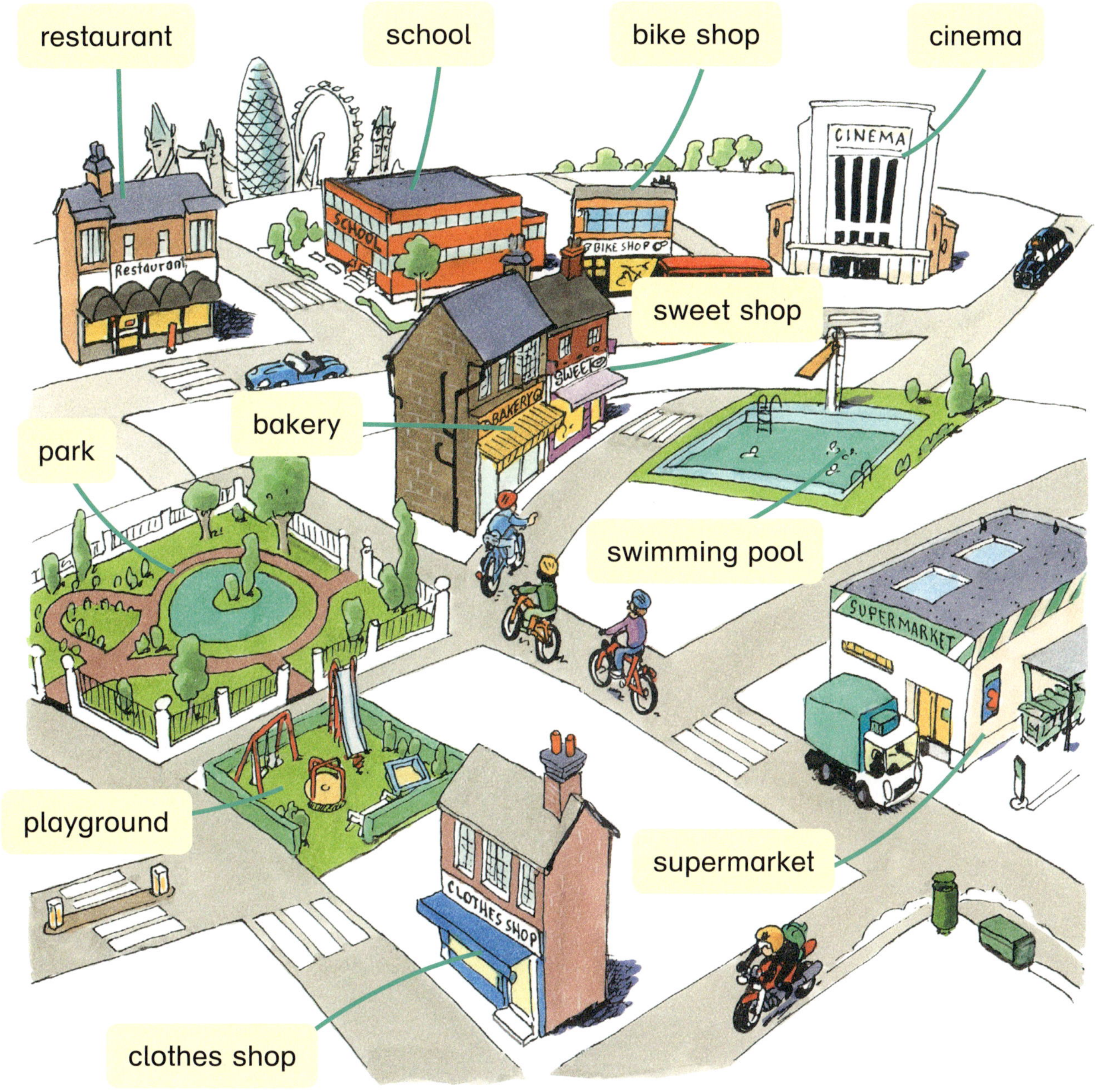

There is a …

I like the **swimming pool**.

Seasons and weather

I like Easter – eating Easter eggs and hot cross buns. Yummy!

In the summer holidays I love making sandcastles at the beach.

spring

summer

autumn

winter

In autumn I like jumping in puddles.

What do I do in winter? Go ice-skating!

A

a/an	ein, eine
a bit	ein bisschen
about	über
ache	der Schmerz, die Schmerzen
+advert	die Werbung
+after	danach
afternoon	der Nachmittag
alarm	der Alarm
alien	der/die Außerirdische
all	alle
all year round	das ganze Jahr hindurch
+also	auch, außerdem
always	immer
and	und
animal	das Tier
to answer	(be)antworten
+any	irgendeine(r, s)
Anything else?	Sonst noch etwas?
apple	der Apfel
apple crumble	der Apfelstreusel-kuchen
+appointment	der Termin
April	der April
April fool!	April April!
arm	der Arm
around	herum, umher
art	die Kunst
art club	die Kunst-AG
as	wie
as well	auch
to ask	fragen
astronaut	der Astronaut/die Astronautin
at	auf, an, in, bei; um
August	der August
aunt/auntie	die Tante
autumn	der Herbst
axe	die Axt

B

back	zurück; der Rücken; die Rückseite
back brake	die Rückbremse
back light	das Rücklicht
back wheel	das Hinterrad
backache	die Rückenschmerzen
bad	schlecht; schlimm
+bag	die Tasche
+to bake	backen
bakery	die Bäckerei
balloon	der (Luft)ballon
banana	die Banane
basket	der Korb
bathroom	das Bad(ezimmer)
beach	der Strand
because	weil
bed	das Bett
bedroom	das Schlafzimmer
bee	die Biene
bell	die Klingel
best	beste(r, s)
big	groß
bike	das Fahrrad
bike shop	das Fahrradgeschäft
bird	der Vogel
birthday	der Geburtstag
black	schwarz
to blow out	ausblasen
blue	blau
+boat	das Boot
bonfire	das (Freuden)feuer
book	das Buch
boot	der Stiefel
boy	der Junge
brake	die Bremse
bread	das Brot

schwarz = *neue Wörter in CMJ 4;* + = *Wörter aus dem optionalen* [+]*-Teil;*
grau = *Wörter aus CMJ 3*

breakfast	das Frühstück
+bricks	die Bauklötze
bright	hell, leuchtend
British	britisch
brochure	die Broschüre
brother	der Bruder
brown	braun
to brush	bürsten, putzen
bucket	der Eimer
bug	der Käfer
to build	(auf)bauen
+bunk bed	das Etagenbett
but	aber
butter	die Butter, buttern
to buy	kaufen
bye	tschüss

C

cake	der Kuchen
+to call	anrufen, nennen
called	namens, genannt
camera	der Fotoapparat
can	können
candle	die Kerze
+car	das Auto
card	die Karte
carrot	die Karotte, die Möhre
to carve	schnitzen
cat	die Katze
+centre	das Zentrum, die Mitte
chair	der Stuhl
+character	der Charakter; die Figur
cheese	der Käse
+chef	der Koch/die Köchin
chest of drawers	die Kommode
chicken	das Huhn
child, children	das Kind, die Kinder
chocolate	die Schokolade
choir	der Chor
to choose	(aus)wählen
cinema	das Kino
city	die Stadt
class	die Klasse
class trip	die Klassenreise, der Schulausflug
classroom	das Klassenzimmer
+claw	die Klaue, die Kralle
+to click one's fingers	(mit den Fingern) schnippen
clock	die Uhr
+close	nah(e)
clothes	die Kleider; die Kleidung
coach	der Trainer/die Trainerin
cold	kalt; die Erkältung
+to collect	sammeln
colour	die Farbe
coloured pencil	der Buntstift
to come	kommen
conker	die (Ross)kastanie
correct	richtig, korrekt
to count	zählen
cousin	der Cousin/die Cousine
cow	die Kuh
+crocodile	das Krokodil
crumble	der Auflauf; der Streusel
+cucumber	die Gurke
+to cut	schneiden

D

to dance	tanzen
+dark	dunkel
date	die Verabredung
day	der Tag
+daytime	der Tag; die Tageszeit
December	der Dezember
dental floss	die Zahnseide
dentist	der Zahnarzt/die Zahnärztin
desk	der Schreibtisch
dialogue	das Gespräch, der Dialog

schwarz = neue Wörter in CMJ 4; + = Wörter aus dem optionalen [+]-Teil; grau = Wörter aus CMJ 3

dictionary .... das Wörterbuch
different .... anders; verschieden
dinner .... das Mittagessen; das Abendessen
+dinosaur .... der Dinosaurier
+dish .... die Backform
to do .... machen, tun
dog .... der Hund
+dolphin .... der Delfin
door .... die Tür
down .... (he)runter
drama club .... die Theater-AG
to draw .... zeichnen
dream .... der Traum
to dribble .... dribbeln
to drink .... trinken
dry .... trocken
duck .... die Ente

E

ear .... das Ohr
earache .... die Ohrenschmerzen
early .... früh
earth .... die Erde
Easter .... Ostern, das Osterfest
to eat .... essen
egg .... das Ei
eight .... acht
eleven .... elf
English .... Englisch; englisch
every .... jede(r, s)
+everything .... alles
excited .... aufgeregt
eye .... das Auge

F

face .... das Gesicht
fact file .... der Steckbrief
fair .... fair, gerecht
to fall .... fallen
family .... die Familie
far away .... weit weg
farmer .... der Bauer/die Bäuerin
fast .... schnell
father/dad .... der Vater, der Papa
favourite .... der Liebling, Lieblings-
February .... der Februar
to feel .... (sich) fühlen
+festival .... das Fest; das Festival
+to fight .... (be)kämpfen
+filling .... die Füllung
to find .... finden
fine .... gut
finger .... der Finger
fire .... das Feuer
fire engine .... das Feuerwehrauto
fire station .... die Feuerwache
firefighter .... der Feuerwehrmann/die Feuerwehrfrau
+first .... erste(r, s), zuerst, als Erstes
fish .... der Fisch
five .... fünf
flame .... die Flamme
+flat .... flach
+floor .... der Boden
+flour .... das Mehl
flower .... die Blume
+to fly .... fliegen
+flyer .... der Flyer, der Werbezettel
foggy .... neblig
+to fold .... falten
folder .... der Ordner, der Schnellhefter
to follow .... folgen
food .... das Essen, die Nahrung(smittel)
+food stall .... der Imbissstand
football .... der Fußball

schwarz = *neue Wörter in CMJ 4;* + = *Wörter aus dem optionalen* ⊞*-Teil;*
grau = *Wörter aus CMJ 3*

football kit .... die Fußballausrüstung
+for .... für
four .... vier
free .... frei
Friday .... der Freitag
friend .... der Freund/ die Freundin
from .... von; aus
front brake .... die Vorderradbremse
front light .... das Vorderlicht
front wheel .... das Vorderrad
frosty .... frostig
fruit .... die Frucht
full moon .... der Vollmond
fun .... der Spaß
funny .... lustig, witzig
furniture .... die Möbel

G

game .... das Spiel
garage .... die Garage
gardening club .... die Garten-AG
gas planet .... der gasförmige Planet
gently .... sanft
to get .... erhalten, bekommen
to get up .... aufstehen
giant .... der Riese/die Riesin
girl .... das Mädchen
to give .... geben
glass .... das Glas
glove .... der Handschuh
glue .... der Klebstoff, der Kleber
to go .... gehen
to go together .... zusammenpassen
goal .... das Ziel; das Tor
goalkeeper .... der Tormann/ die Torfrau
+going to .... werden
good .... gut
Good Friday .... der Karfreitag
Good morning! .... Guten Morgen!
Goodbye! .... Auf Wiedersehen!
grandfather/ grandpa .... der Großvater, der Opa
grandmother/ grandma .... die Großmutter, die Oma
great .... wunderbar; groß
green .... grün
grey .... grau
ground .... der (Erd)boden
to guess .... (er)raten
guest .... der Gast
guinea pig .... das Meerschweinchen
guitar .... die Gitarre

H

half past (four) .... halb (fünf)
hall .... der Flur, der Korridor
ham .... der Schinken
hamster .... der Hamster
hand .... die Hand; der (Uhr)Zeiger
+to happen .... geschehen, passieren
happy .... glücklich; fröhlich
Happy Birthday! .... Alles Gute zum Geburtstag!
hard .... hart
hat .... der Hut, die Mütze
+to hate .... hassen, verabscheuen
to have .... haben
have got .... haben
he .... er
head .... der Kopf
headache .... das Kopfweh, die Kopfschmerzen
healthy .... gesund
to hear .... hören
helmet .... der Helm
her .... ihr(e)

schwarz = neue Wörter in CMJ 4; + = Wörter aus dem optionalen [+]-Teil; grau = Wörter aus CMJ 3

+here	hier
Here you are.	Bitte sehr.
his	sein(e, r)
holiday	der Urlaub, die Ferien
+hollow	hohl
home	das Zuhause
homework	die Hausaufgaben
+to hop	hüpfen, hopsen
+horn	das Horn
horse	das Pferd
horse-riding	das Reiten
hose	der Schlauch
hot	heiß
+hour	die Stunde
house	das Haus
to hurry up	sich beeilen

I

I	ich
ice hockey	das Eishockey
ice-skating	das Schlittschuhfahren, das Eislaufen
idea	die Idee
if	wenn, falls
important	wichtig
in	in
+in front of	vor
in the end	am Ende, am Schluss
inside	in, drinnen, innen
+interesting	interessant
to interview	interviewen
invitation	die Einladung
+it	es; er/sie/es
+its	sein(e), ihr(e)

J

jacket	die Jacke
January	der Januar
joke	der Witz
juice	der Saft
July	der Juli
to jump	springen, hüpfen
June	der Juni
+Jupiter	der Jupiter

K

to keep away	fernhalten
+kilo	das Kilo
+kind	die Art, die Sorte
+king	der König
kitchen	die Küche
knee	das Knie
to know	wissen; kennen

L

ladder	die Leiter
to land	landen
last	letzte(r, s)
late	(zu) spät
later	später
+leaf, leaves	das Blatt, die Blätter
leg	das Bein
lemonade	die (Zitronen)limo(nade)
lesson	die Unterrichtsstunde
let's (= let us)	lass(t) uns
letter	der Brief
+lettuce	der Salat, der Kopfsalat
to light	anzünden
lighter	das Feuerzeug
like	mögen
list	die Liste
to listen (to)	(zu)hören
living room	das Wohnzimmer
in their lives	in ihrem ganzen Leben
loo	das Klo
to look	schauen, sehen
+to lose	verlieren
I lost my tooth.	Ich habe meinen Zahn verloren.

schwarz = *neue Wörter in CMJ 4;* + = *Wörter aus dem optionalen* ⊞*-Teil;*
grau = *Wörter aus CMJ 3*

lots of ..... viel(e), jede Menge
loud ..... laut
to love ..... lieben, sehr mögen
lunch ..... das Mittagessen

M

to make ..... machen
man ..... der Mann
many ..... viele
March ..... der März
+Mars ..... der Mars
to match (with) ..... zuordnen
maths (= mathematics) ..... die Mathematik
May ..... der Mai
me ..... mir, mich
meat ..... das Fleisch
+meat-eater ..... der Fleischfresser
to meet ..... (sich) treffen
+menu ..... die Speisekarte
+Mercury ..... der Merkur
mess ..... das Durcheinander
+metre ..... der Meter
milk ..... die Milch
+million ..... die Million
to mix ..... (ver)mischen
+model ..... das Modell
Monday ..... der Montag
money ..... das Geld
month ..... der Monat
moon ..... der Mond
+more ..... (noch) mehr
morning ..... der Morgen
mother/mum ..... die Mutter, die Mama
mouse ..... die Maus
mouth ..... der Mund
+much ..... viel; sehr
muesli ..... das Müsli
music ..... die Musik
must ..... müssen
my ..... mein(e)

N

to need ..... brauchen
neighbourhood ..... das Stadtviertel, der Stadtteil
+Neptune ..... der Neptun
never ..... nie(mals)
new ..... neu
new moon ..... der Neumond
+night ..... die Nacht; der Abend
+nighttime ..... die Nacht
nine ..... neun
no ..... nein
nose ..... die Nase
+not ..... nicht
November ..... der November
number ..... die Zahl; die Nummer
nut ..... die Nuss

O

o'clock ..... (neun) Uhr
October ..... der Oktober
often ..... oft
old ..... alt
on ..... auf; an
once a day ..... einmal am Tag
one ..... eins; ein(e)
only ..... nur
open ..... offen, geöffnet
to open ..... öffnen
+open day ..... der Tag der offenen Tür
+or ..... oder
orange ..... orange(farben)
orange juice ..... der Orangensaft
+other ..... andere(r, s)
our ..... unsere(r, s)
out of ..... aus
+oven ..... der Ofen
+over ..... über

schwarz = neue Wörter in CMJ 4; + = Wörter aus dem optionalen [+]-Teil; grau = Wörter aus CMJ 3

P

to pack	packen
page	die Seite
pancake	der Pfannkuchen
+paper	das Papier
park	der Park
parrot	der Papagei
have a party	eine Party feiern
pea	die Erbse
pen	der Stift
pencil	der Bleistift
pencil case	die Federtasche
pencil sharpener	der (An)spitzer
+people	die Leute, die Menschen
pet	das Haustier
+petrol station	die Tankstelle
+photo	das Bild, das Foto
picture	das Bild
pig	das Schwein
pink	pink, rosa
+place	der Platz
+to plan	planen
planet	der Planet
+plant	die Pflanze
+plant-eater	der Pflanzenfresser
+plate	der Teller
to play	spielen
to play a trick	einen Streich spielen
playground	der Spielplatz; der Schulhof
please	bitte
poem	das Gedicht
to point	zeigen
+poison	das Gift
+poisonous	giftig
pole	die Stange
+poo	das Kacka
pound	das Pfund
present	das Geschenk
to present	präsentieren
pretty	hübsch, schön
+programme	das Programm
to protect	schützen
+pudding	die Nachspeise
puddle	die Pfütze
pumpkin	der Kürbis
purple	violett, lila(farben)

Q

quarter to (five)	Viertel vor (fünf)
quarter past (four)	Viertel nach (vier)
quiz	das Quiz

R

rabbit	das Kaninchen
rain	der Regen
raindrop	der Regentropfen
rainy	regnerisch
to read	lesen
really	wirklich
+recipe	das Rezept
red	rot
reflector	der Rückstrahler, der Reflektor
to remember	sich erinnern (an)
restaurant	das Restaurant
ride	die Fahrt
to ride a bike	Fahrrad fahren
+right	richtig
+ring	der Ring
+rocky	felsig, steinig
room	das Zimmer
round	rund
rubber	der Radiergummi
+rug	der Teppich
ruler	das Lineal
to run	rennen, laufen

S

sad	traurig

schwarz = *neue Wörter in CMJ 4;* + = *Wörter aus dem optionalen* ⊞*-Teil;*
grau = *Wörter aus CMJ 3*

saddle	der Sattel
+salad	der Salat
+salt	das Salz
sandcastle	die Sandburg
+sandwich	das Sandwich
Saturday	der Samstag
+Saturn	der Saturn
sausage	die Wurst, das Würstchen
+scared	verängstigt
scary	unheimlich
school	die Schule
school club	die Schul-Arbeitsgemeinschaft, die Schul-AG
school uniform	die Schuluniform
schoolbag	die Schultasche, der Ranzen
science club	die Naturwissenschaftliche AG
scissors	die Schere
season	die Jahreszeit
+second	die Sekunde
to see	sehen
+sentence	der Satz
September	der September
seven	sieben
+shark	der Hai(fisch)
+she	sie
sheep	das Schaf
+sheet	das Laken; das Blatt (Papier)
shelf	das Regal
shirt	das Hemd
shoe	der Schuh
shop	der Laden
shopping	das Einkaufen
shopping list	die Einkaufsliste
sick	krank
+side	die Seite
to sing	singen
sister	die Schwester
to sit	sitzen
six	sechs
skiing	das Skifahren
sky	der Himmel
sledging	das Schlittenfahren
+slice	die Scheibe
slide down	herunterrutschen
small	klein
to smell	riechen, duften
+snake	die Schlange
snow	der Schnee
snow angel	der Schneeengel
snowball fight	die Schneeballschlacht
snowman	der Schneemann
snowy	schneereich
so	so; deshalb; also
sock	die Socke
+solar system	das Sonnensystem
some	etwas; einige
+something	etwas
sometimes	manchmal
song	das Lied
soon	bald
sorry	Entschuldigung
sound	der Klang; das Geräusch
space	der Weltraum
space shuttle	die (Welt)raumfähre, das Spaceshuttle
spaceship	das Raumschiff
special	besondere(r, s)
+to spread	(be)streichen; verteilen
spring	der Frühling
+to sprinkle	(be)streuen
star	der Stern
start	der Anfang
+stopwatch	die Stoppuhr

schwarz = neue Wörter in CMJ 4; + = Wörter aus dem optionalen [+]-Teil; grau = Wörter aus CMJ 3

story ... die Geschichte
street ... die Straße
+strong ... stark, kräftig
+sugar ... der Zucker
summer ... der Sommer
summertime ... die Sommerzeit
sun ... die Sonne
Sunday ... der Sonntag
+sunlight ... das Sonnenlicht
sunny ... sonnig
sunshine ... der Sonnenschein
supermarket ... der Supermarkt
surprise ... die Überraschung
sweet ... die Süßigkeit
to swim ... schwimmen

T

table ... der Tisch
table tennis ... das Tischtennis
tail ... der Schwanz
to take ... nehmen; dauern
to talk ... sprechen, reden
tea ... der Tee
to tell ... erzählen, sagen
+temperature ... die Temperatur
ten ... zehn
test ... der Test, die Prüfung
text ... der Text
+than ... als
thank you ... danke
the ... der/die/das
the same ... der-/die-/dasselbe; gleich
+their ... ihr(e)
+them ... sie, ihnen
+then ... dann
there ... dort, da
there is, there are ... es gibt, da sind
+they ... sie
thing ... das Ding, der Gegenstand
thirty ... dreißig
+this ... diese(r, s); das
three ... drei
through ... durch
Thursday ... der Donnerstag
tick-tock ... ticktack
+to tidy ... aufräumen
time ... die Zeit; die Uhrzeit
today ... heute
toe ... der Zeh
tomato, tomatoes ... die Tomate, die Tomaten
+ton ... die Tonne
+too ... auch
tooth fairy ... die Zahnfee
tooth, teeth ... der Zahn, die Zähne
toothache ... die Zahnschmerzen
toothbrush ... die Zahnbürste
toothpaste ... die Zahnpasta
torch ... die Taschenlampe
+tower ... der Turm
town ... die Stadt
+toy ... das Spielzeug
+traffic light ... die Ampel
tree ... der Baum
trick ... der Trick, das Kunststück
trolley ... der Einkaufswagen
trousers ... die Hose
Tuesday ... der Dienstag
tummy ... der Bauch
tummy ache ... das Bauchweh
twelve ... zwölf
two ... zwei
tyre ... der Reifen

U

uncle ... der Onkel
under ... unter

schwarz = *neue Wörter in CMJ 4;* + = *Wörter aus dem optionalen* [+]*-Teil;*
grau = *Wörter aus CMJ 3*

+up to ... bis (zu)
+Uranus ... der Uranus
+us ... uns
to use ... (be)nutzen

V
+vanilla ... die Vanille
vegetable ... das Gemüse
+Venus ... die Venus
very ... sehr

W
to wait ... warten; abwarten
to wake up ... aufwachen
to walk ... (spazieren) gehen
to want ... wollen
wardrobe ... der (Kleider)schrank
to wash ... waschen
to watch ... beobachten, zusehen
water ... das Wasser
wave ... die Welle
we ... wir
to wear ... tragen, anhaben
weather forecast ... der Wetterbericht
Wednesday ... der Mittwoch
week ... die Woche
weekend ... das Wochenende
+to weigh ... wiegen
+welcome ... Willkommen
well done! ... gut gemacht!
wellies ... die Gummistiefel
what ... was; welche(r, s)
What's wrong? ... Was ist los?/ Wo ist das Problem?
What would you like? Was möchtest du?
wheel ... das Rad
when ... wenn
where ... wo; wohin
which ... welche(r, s)
white ... weiß
who ... wer
why ... warum
+wide ... weit
+will ... werden
+window ... das Fenster
windy ... windig
winter ... der Winter
wish ... der Wunsch
to wish ... wünschen
with ... mit
wobbly ... wack(e)lig
wool ... die Wolle
word ... das Wort
word web ... das Wortnetz
+work ... die Arbeit
+to work ... arbeiten
to worry ... sich Sorgen machen
would like ... möchte (gern)
+to write ... schreiben
wrong ... falsch

Y
year ... das Jahr
yellow ... gelb
yes ... ja
yesterday ... gestern
yoghurt ... das Jogurt
you ... du, dich, dir, Sie, Ihnen; ihr, euch; man
your ... dein(e); euer/eure; Ihr(e)
yummy ... lecker

Z
zoo ... der Zoo
zebra crossing ... der Zebrastreifen

schwarz = *neue Wörter in CMJ 4;* + = *Wörter aus dem optionalen* ⊞*-Teil;*
grau = *Wörter aus CMJ 3*

Bildquellen

|Alamy Stock Photo, Abingdon/Oxfordshire: Ascannio 40.2. |Alamy Stock Photo (RMB), Abingdon/Oxfordshire: du Feu, Geoff 79.2; Jack Sullivan 81.2; Robert Slade 61.1; Teare, Jeanette 40.5. |Amortegui, Miguel, Saltdean - Rottingdean: 10.1, 14.1, 14.2, 14.3, 14.4, 14.5, 14.6, 14.7, 19.5, 22.2, 23.2, 23.4, 30.1, 39.1, 39.2, 39.3, 40.1, 64.1, 68.2, 81.1. |dreamstime.com, Brentwood: York, James 21.2. |Focus Photo- u. Presseagentur GmbH, Hamburg: Focus Network Photographers, Homer Skyes 79.1. |fotolia.com, New York: fffranz 9.1, 9.2, 9.3, 9.4, 86.1, 86.2, 86.3, 86.4; Syda Productions 72.1; Woodapple 75.1. |Getty Images, München: 53.3. |Hamill, Aisling, Braunschweig: 12.2, 50.1, 72.2, 80.1. |Hammersen-Schiffner, Bettina, Braunschweig: 9.5, 9.6, 9.7, 17.1, 18.1, 26.1, 39.4, 39.5, 39.6, 48.1, 60.2. |Harder, Katrin, Berlin: 73.1, 73.2, 73.3, 74.1, 74.2, 74.3. |Hommel, Mirja, Frankfurt/M.: 15.1. |iStockphoto.com, Calgary: 13.1, 40.3, 40.4, 40.6; Andrew Howe 34.2; Bakai 4.1, 4.2, 11.2, 14.8, 21.1, 24.3, 31.1, 34.3, 38.1, 41.1, 49.1, 53.7, 60.1, 65.2, 68.1; baona 78.3; Christian Martínez Kempin 34.1; evgenyatamanenko 78.4; FatCamera Titel; hazel proudlove 83.1; Highwaystarz-Photography 22.1; Issaurinko 12.1; Pepgooner 42.1; rwarnick 24.1, 24.2; Steve Stone 23.3; sturti 23.1; tatyana_tomsickova 78.2. |Koerner, Amy, Frankfurt am Main: 29.1, 35.1, 35.3, 45.1, 45.2, 52.1, 64.2, 65.1, 70.1. |Kömür, Demet: 19.1, 19.2, 19.3, 19.4, 25.1, 25.2, 25.3, 62.1, 62.2, 62.3, 62.4, 75.2, 75.3, 83.2. |laif, Köln: GAMMA 53.5. |mauritius images GmbH, Mittenwald: Alamy / Ryder, Lisa 85.1; Mint Images 78.1. |Naumann, Andrea, Aachen: 42.2. |Nazirizadeh, Yousef, Frankfurt: 11.1, 55.1, 55.2. |Nungesser, Verena-Susanna, Stuttgart: Amy Koerner, Portsmouth 35.2. |Picture-Alliance GmbH, Frankfurt/M.: dpa 21.3. |Schneider, Barbara, Bremen: 53.1, 53.2. |Shutterstock.com, New York: mrjo 53.6; Pannochka 53.4. |Shutterstock.com (RM), New York: hsvrs 78.5. |The Travel Library, Berlin: Andy Williams 79.3.

Textquellen

13 "I'm late" from Walt Disney's *Alice in Wonderland*. Words by Bob Hilliard, Music by Sammy Fain © 1949 Walt Disney Music Company. Copyrights Renewed. All Rights Reserved. Used by Permission. Reprinted by Permission of Hal Leonard Corporation.

CAMDEN MARKET
JUNIOR

CD1 – TEXTBOOK

Intro 1/2 Back to school

Theme 1: Around the clock
3 a) The first day of school
4 c) The first day of school
5/6 Ruby, you're late!
7 Ruby's clocks
8/9 Tick tock
10 Clocks, clocks, clocks
11/12 What time is it?
13 Rajiv's day
14 The six-dinner cat
15 The White Rabbit

Theme 2: School clubs
16 A school club for David
17 c) The perfect school club
18 School clubs
19 Football club
20 At science club
21 The moon
22 David in space
23/24 The earth turns around
25 Ruby's tongue twisters

Theme 3: Birthdays
26 Karla is excited!
27 +WB Birthday ideas
28 Birthdays
29 A birthday invitation
30 Birthday words
31 Karla's birthday party
32/33 Birthday song
34 +WB A very special day
35 +WB Liam's birthday surprise
36/37 A birthday chant
38 Ruby's tongue twisters
39 a) Meet the dinosaurs
40 c) Meet the dinosaurs
41/42 Thomas and Catherine's day at the museum

Theme 4: What we eat and drink
43 At the supermarket
44/45 Trolley chant
46 What we eat and drink
47 a) Numbers
48 b) Numbers
49 At the farmer's market
50 The giant called Ed
51/52 Carrots, peas and broccoli

Theme 5: At the dentist
53 +WB I don't feel well!
54 What's wrong?
55 +WB David at the dentist
56 Captain Neverland's teeth
57 Rhyming words

CD2 – TEXTBOOK

Theme 6: At the fire station
1 In Ben's home
2 In the rooms
3 At the fire station
4 +WB Fire station words
5 What a firefighter needs
6/7 +WB Down at the fire station
8 Inside the fire station
9 Freddie the firefighter
10 Ruby's tongue twisters
11 My room: Catherine
12 My room: Thomas

Theme 7: In the city
13 a) David's street
14 c) David's street
15 What a cool bike!
16/17 +WB Bike chant
18 At the bike shop
19 a) In the neighbourhood
20 +WB c) In the neighbourhood
21 Emily's bike

Theme 8: All year round
22 +WB Weather forecast: Autumn
23 +WB Weather forecast: Winter
24 +WB Weather forecast: Spring
25 +WB Weather forecast: Summer
26 November
27 We love autumn!
28/29 It's Bonfire Night!
30 Winter chant
31 The snow falls gently
32 A pancake party at …
33/34 Spring is here!
35 April fool!
36 +WB Easter at Karla's house
37 In the summertime
38 Plans for the summer
39 The last day of term

CD2 – WORKBOOK

Theme 1: Around the clock
40 Late, late, late
41 Clocks
42 Test yourself 1

Theme 2: School clubs
43 Which school club is it?
44 Our school clubs
45 The earth turns around
46 An alien says hello
47 Test yourself 1
48 The planets

Theme 3: Birthdays
49 Months of the year
50 A birthday invitation
51 What is in the parcel?
52 Test yourself 1

Theme 4: What we eat and drink
53 Which trolley?
54 Often, sometimes, never
55 Which number?
56 Test yourself 1

Theme 5: At the dentist
57 A telephone call
58 Test yourself 1

Theme 6: At the fire station
59 Rooms
60 Mr Miller's team
61 Test yourself 1
62 Room poems

Theme 7: In the city
63 At the bike shop
64 Test yourself 1

Theme 8: All year round
65-68 Weather chants (Autumn, Winter Spring, Summer)
69 Autumn poem
70 The best Bonfire Night ever
71 How do you like your pancakes?